150

THINGS TO MAKE AND DO WITH YOUR CHILDREN

JULIET MOXLEY

IN ASSOCIATION WITH

SHE
MAGAZINE

LIMITED EDITIONS
BOOKTITLES

For Mark and V. J. Lowe

This edition published in 1994 by Limited Editions
by arrangement with Vermilion
an imprint of Ebury Press
Random House
20 Vauxhall Bridge Road
London SW1V 2SA

A catalogue record for this book is
available from the British Library

ISBN 0 09 182512 1

Edited by Cindy Richards
Designed by Jerry Goldie

Typeset in Bookman & Futura by Textype Typesetters, Cambridge
Printed and bound in Portugal by Printer Portuguesa Lda
Colour separations by Magnacraft using environmentally friendly inks.
Papers used by Ebury Press are natural recyclable products made
from wood grown in sustainable forests. In addition, the paper in this
book is acid free.

Acknowledgements

The author and publishers wish to thank the following people for
making this book possible:
All the Children at Highfield School and Nursery, 256 Trinity Road,
Wandsworth Common, London SW18 3RQ
The following children, who also modelled : Geoffrey Elston, Fiona
Fullerton, Oliver Holstrom, Alice Hobbs, Sasha Haworth, Jay
Haworth, Jennifer May, Jessica and Alice Moxley, Mimi Newman
and Matthew Plowright. Lucy Tizard for taking the photographs. The
staff of Highfield School for letting me disrupt the school for a week!
Jill Sheridan who sorted out my manuscript and Cindy Richards who
edited it. Alice Wilson, Sean Murphy, Innez Murphy, Jessica Moxley
and Monica Syversen who made things for the book.
The following stockists who supplied materials for free: Inscribe for
fabric paints and Fimo, Dylon for fabric pens and dyes, Pelikan for
specialist papers, modelling materials, pens and paints, Pebeo for
fabric pens, 3M for sticky tapes, Henkel for pritt stick and copydex,
Fablon for sticky-backed plastics, Fruit of the Loom for T-shirts,
Offray for ribbons and Creative bead craft for sequins.

Contents

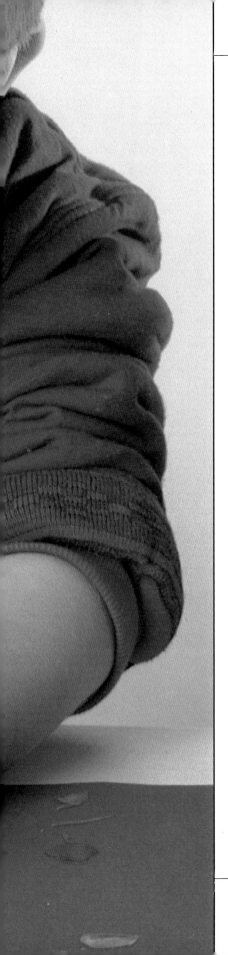

Introduction

150 Things to Make and Do with Your Children is a book of ideas. It is hopefully the place where you can look when your child says once again 'Mum I'm bored'.

The book includes activities for all ages and for children with different abilities. Although some projects include materials which may be expensive to buy, many are inexpensive and use materials and equipment normally found in the home. Some of the most exciting craft projects are made from the cheapest materials, my own favourites are papier mâché and salt dough. Both of these materials may be used by the youngest and the oldest age groups, although a two-year-old will need more assistance with papier mâché than a twelve-year-old.

The book has been divided into sections to make it easier to use: Drawing and Painting, Modelling, Crafting, Fun with Food, Growing Things, Outdoor Pursuits, and a special section on Easter and Christmas. Many of the ideas are old favourites with a new twist whilst others are quite unusual. All the items in the book have been consumer tested by children ranging from one to thirteen. My own children aged thirteen, eleven, six and twenty months have all been involved in the making of this book and have had great fun making, doing and sometimes eating the projects. Always remember to supervise all activities that require the use of knives, scissors or ovens.

I hope you have fun using this book.

Juliet Moxley

CHAPTER ONE

DRAWING AND PAINTING

This section of the book covers a range of techniques from the simplest – bubble and leaf printing – through to the more sophisticated such as making stencils.

Make sure you and your child are wearing suitable clothing – aprons or old shirts are a must – and that your work area is protected when painting and printing. You will also need a drying area and always remember to wash brushes after use. This is easy to do while the paint is wet but not once it has dried. Acrylic paint is particularly difficult to remove. One of the cheapest ways of obtaining drawing and painting paper is to buy rolls of lining paper or to draw on the back of left over rolls of wallpaper. Remember to supervise any cutting, or do it yourself if younger children are involved.

Hand and Foot Printing

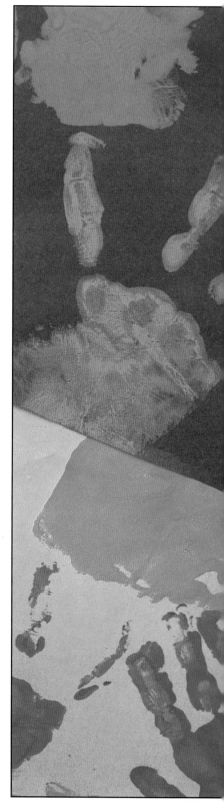

A good way to decorate large areas, hand and foot printing can be used to make a frieze or, by cutting out the individual prints and sticking them on another background, an attractive montage.

YOU WILL NEED
Newspaper
Large piece of plain paper on which to make prints
Masking tape
Poster or powder paint
Container for paint
Thick brush
Bowl of water to wash hands and feet
Towel

1 Cover a large area of the floor with newspaper.

2 Use masking tape to attach the plain paper to the newspaper.

3 Mix some paint in the container and then paint hand with the brush.

4 Press down your hand on the paper to transfer the paint from your hand to the paper.

5 Continue this process until you have a series of handprints on the paper.

6 When finished, wash your hand in the bowl of water and dry thoroughly.

7 Repeat the process using a different coloured paint.

You can use the same technique to make prints of your feet. Make sure your prints are clear by washing and drying your feet each time you make a print.

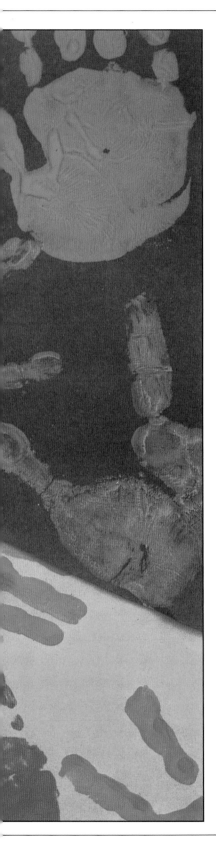

Fingerpainting

Children love finger painting and can use a lot of paint in one session so here are a few simple recipes. It is also very messy so make sure they cover up well.

RECIPE 1
Water
Flour
Food colouring
Bowl
Spoon

1 Put equal quantities of water and flour into a bowl.

2 Add colouring.

RECIPE 2
Wallpaper paste
Dry powder paint
Spoon
Empty washing-up-liquid bottles with the tops cut off

1 Mix the wallpaper paste according to the instructions on the packet.

2 Pour the paste into the bottles.

3 Add some dry powder paint to each bottle and mix with a spoon.

RECIPE 3
1 cup of soap powder
½ cup water
Food colouring (1 capful) or powder paint
Bowl
Spoon

1 Place all the ingredients in a bowl and mix them together with a spoon until the mixture reaches a stiff consistency.

RECIPE 4
1 cup cornflour
Water – enough to dissolve cornflour
Kettle of boiling water
1 cup soapflakes
Powder paint or food colouring
A large saucepan
Spoon
Empty ice-cream or margarine tubs

1 Add the cornflour to a little water. Warm this mixture over a low heat until the cornflour dissolves.

2 Add the boiling water.

3 Stir until the mixture thickens.

4 Remove from the heat and add soapflakes.

5 Leave the mixture to cool.

6 Pour into the empty containers and add a different coloured paint or food colouring to each one.

Leaf Printing

This is a fun activity to do after a walk when you have collected as many different varieties of leaves as possible.

YOU WILL NEED
Newspaper
Paper on which to print
Containers (one for each colour paint)
Powder or poster paint
Thick brush
Leaves

1 Cover your work surface with newspaper and place your printing paper on top.

2 Pour some paint into the container.

3 Select a leaf and paint one side.

4 Carefully place the painted side of the leaf onto the paper and press it down firmly ensuring pressure is applied to the whole surface.

5 Remove the leaf and repeat steps 3 and 4 until the desired pattern has been achieved.

It is advisable to use only one colour per leaf. If you use more, the colours will mix and become muddy.

Alternatives
● Draw around the leaves and colour in the shapes with paint.

Making Textures and Patterns

A great variety of patterns and textures can be easily created by applying paint using a range of unusual but everyday household items.

YOU WILL NEED
Newspaper
Paper
Watercolour or poster paints
Wide paintbrush
Saucer
Sponge
Cork
Comb
Toothbrush
Kitchen roll
Knitted fabric
Different sized paintbrushes
Feather
Pastry cutters

Sponge Painting

1 Pour some paint into a saucer.

2 Dip the sponge into paint and dab it onto the paper.

3 Wash sponge and repeat the process using another colour.

Alternative Sponge Pattern

1 Cover the paper with paint using the wide paintbrush.

2 Using a dry sponge, dab it across the painted surface. The dry sponge will remove some paint creating an interesting pattern.

Cork Pattern

1 Again using the wide paintbrush, cover the paper with paint.

2 When the paint is almost dry, take a cork and roll it over the paper.

Combing Pattern

1 Cover the paper with paint using the brush.

2 Take the comb and gently drag it through the wet paint being careful not to rip the wet paper.

Note: A similar but finer texture can be achieved using a toothbrush.

Kitchen Roll Painting

1 Using the brush, cover the paper in paint.

2 Take a piece of kitchen roll and scrunch it up into a loose ball.

3 Dab it across the painted paper and a pattern will emerge as the kitchen roll absorbs some of the wet paint.

Knitted Fabric Painting

1 Pour some paint into a saucer.

2 Take a piece of knitted fabric, such as an old glove or part of an old jumper, and dip it into the paint.

3 Dab the fabric onto the paper and a pattern will emerge.

4 Repeat the process using a feather instead of the knitted fabric to create another interesting effect.

Spatter Printing

1 Cover a large area of your work surface with old newspaper.

2 Dip one of the brushes into the paint and then flick the brush so that the paint spatters across the paper.

3 Repeat using different sized brushes and different coloured paints to create a variety of spatter effects.

Pastry Cutter Patterns

1 Place the pastry cutter on some plain paper and draw round it with a pencil.

2 Repeat this several times creating a pattern on the paper.

3 Join the shapes together with painted lines of colour using a paintbrush. The lines will cross over each other to create a lovely interwoven pattern.

4 Colour the shapes and add faces if appropriate.

Bubble Painting

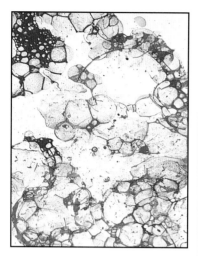

Young children can make very attractive paintings using this simple technique.

YOU WILL NEED
Newspaper
Paper
Washing-up liquid
Powder paint
Empty yoghurt cartons for paint
Thick straws

1 Cover work surface with newspaper.

2 Mix some powder paint with a small amount of water in one of the cartons. Add two tablespoons of washing-up liquid to this mixture. Repeat this process for each colour.

3 Place a straw in the paint mixture and blow until bubbles arise above the top of the carton.

4 Take a piece of paper and place it gently on top of the carton. Move the paper around slowly so that paint from the bubbles is transferred to the paper. If you want a larger area of colour, blow more bubbles.

5 Repeat this process using each colour so you achieve a sheet of multicoloured bubble prints.

Mirror or Butterfly Paintings

This way of creating a picture is very simple and can be enjoyed by younger children. It can be made more interesting for older children by encouraging them to include more details.

YOU WILL NEED
Newspaper
Paper
Paintbrush
Paint

1 Carefully fold the paper exactly in half.

2 Open up the paper and drip paint near the centre fold of the paper.

3 Fold the paper in half and press the sides firmly together.

4 Open out the paper and admire the effect.

Alternatives
● While your mirror painting is still wet make a print of it by pressing it down on another piece of paper.
● Add details to your painting such as feelers and eyes to make it look more like a real butterfly.

Simple Stencilling Using Doilies

This is a simple way to make wrapping paper and requires little skill.

YOU WILL NEED
Newspaper
Plain paper
Paper doilies
Masking tape
Poster paint
Thick brush

1 Cover work surface generously with newspaper.

2 Place the doily over the plain paper and tape it down with masking tape.

3 Hold the brush vertically and stamp the paint onto the paper with an up and down movement.

4 Remove the doily, taking care not to smudge the paint. Allow to dry.

Making a Stencil

Traditionally stencils have been used to create patterned wallpapers, fabrics and wrapping papers because they enable you to repeat a design exactly. If you decide to have a go at making a stencil then do keep your pattern simple as not only will it be easier to cut but simple designs are often more effective.

YOU WILL NEED
Tracing paper
Pencil and black felt-tip pen
Carbon paper
Vinyl, clear acetate or manilla paper for the stencil
Board on which to cut
Craft or Stanley knife
Masking tape

1 Trace the design onto the tracing paper using a pencil.

2 Place the carbon paper between your traced design and the stencil paper. Trace over the design again with the pencil to transfer the marks to the stencil paper.

3 Remove the carbon and tracing paper and go over the outline on the stencil paper with the felt-tip pen to ensure the design is clear.

4 Use the masking tape to attach the stencil paper to the cutting board. Cut out the design using the knife.

Note: The easiest way to cut curved areas is to keep the knife still and to move the stencil paper.

Printing with Stencils

Stencilling looks easier to do than it really is so always take time before starting to think about the effect you wish to achieve. For example, you need to consider how much space to leave before repeating the design and to mark this carefully in pencil on the paper on which you plan to print your designs.

YOU WILL NEED
Stencil
Newspaper
Pencil
Paper on which to print
Paint
Stencil brush
Masking tape

1 Cover your work surface with newspaper. Use the masking tape to secure your printing paper to this surface and then to tape the stencil to this paper.

2 Dip the stencil brush into the paint and remove any excess by stamping the

brush up and down on the newspaper. It is important not to have too much paint on the brush as it will bleed under the edge of the stencil and smudge.

3 Hold the brush vertically and stamp the paint onto the paper with an up and down movement being careful not to move the stencil.

4 Carefully remove the stencil and allow to dry.

5 Repeat this process at set intervals to create a repeat pattern.

Ripped Newspaper Stencil

This is another simple and effective way of stencilling.

YOU WILL NEED
Newspaper
Paper
Masking tape
Saucer
Poster or powder paint
Paintbrush

1 Cover the work surface with newspaper.

2 Tear more newspaper into lengthwise strips. Ensure the torn edges are not too straight by making them wiggle as you rip the paper.

3 Place the newspaper pieces across your printing paper, leaving gaps between each piece. Hold the pieces in place by taping the ends to the newspaper surround.

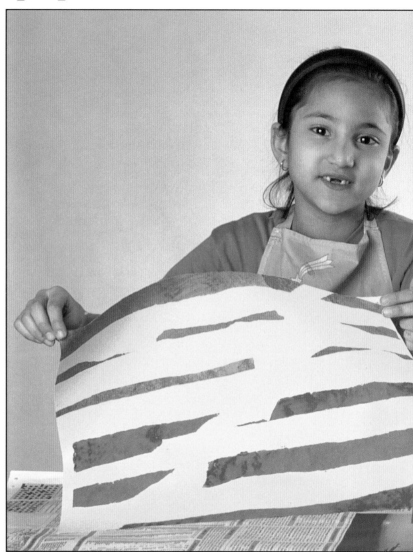

4 Pour some paint into the saucer.

5 Dip the brush into the paint, removing any excess on some spare newspaper.

6 Dab colour onto the paper between the rows of torn newspaper strips ensuring all the paper is covered (*see right*).

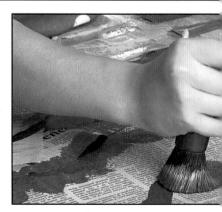

Window Painting

Children find it fascinating to paint on glass especially on their own bedroom windows! Most paint wipes off very easily especially powder and poster paint.

YOU WILL NEED
Newspaper
Masking tape
Paintbrushes
Powder or poster paint

1 Cover any windowsills or other woodwork with newspaper and tape, or just masking tape, to protect them.

2 Mix paint thickly so that the colour is intense as week colours do not show up on glass.

3 Paint simple, bold designs on the inside of the window.

Note: The longer paint is left the more difficult it is to remove.

7 Remove the newspaper strips to reveal the pattern (*see right*).

17

Potato Printing

This method of printing is cheap and easy. You can also use other vegetables, or fruits, such as cauliflowers, peppers, carrots, apples or pears.

YOU WILL NEED
Potatoes
Craft or sharp kitchen knife
Paintbrush
Felt-tip pen
Thick paint
Empty yoghurt cartons for paint or a palette
Paper on which to print

1 Wash the potato and cut it in half.

2 Draw a simple shape on the flat half of the potato with the felt pen.

3 Using the knife, cut away the potato surrounding the shape (ask an adult to do this for you).

4 Pour some paint into the yoghurt carton or palette.

5 Coat the shape with paint using the brush.

6 Press it down onto the paper.

7 Add more paint to the block as the print fades.

Alternatives
● Younger children can have fun using this technique by using the fruit or vegetable cut in half.
● A pattern can be cut into the flat surface of the potato before applying the paint. Using this method the pattern remains white and the background coloured. The results are not quite as crisp as those achieved using a block.

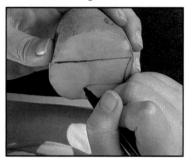

Draw Round a Friend

This is a very straightforward and fun thing to do as long as you have enough space and are well prepared before your start.

YOU WILL NEED
Large sheet of paper or lining paper
Selotape
Chalk or crayons
Scissors
Paintbrushes
Paint

1 Place the paper on the floor ensuring it is larger than the child. (You may have to join several pieces together with tape.)

2 Ask the child to lay face upwards on the paper and draw around his or her body using chalk or crayons.

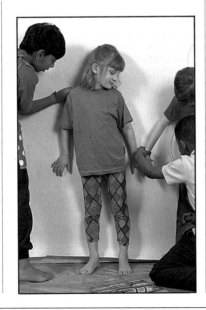

3 Cut out the shape of the child.

4 Cover a large area with newspaper and place the cutout on this.

5 Colour in the cutout using paint or crayons and allow to dry. You can then pin the image to the wall.

Alternatives
• A group of children doing this could hang their images on a wall to create a crowd scene.
• You could tape some paper onto a wall and take turns to stand against it while your friends draw around you. Paint the resulting images.

Making a Backdrop

You will need a large surface on which to create a backdrop so ensure you have cleared a large enough space and prepared everything before beginning this project. It is also fun to undertake a large project like this with a group of friends.

There are several ways of going about making a backdrop: you can either paint directly onto your paper background, as can be seen from the photographs, or cut out objects from newspaper and use them as templates, or you can actually make the objects from paper and stick them onto the backdrop to give a three-dimensional effect.

YOU WILL NEED
Large piece of background paper
(wallpaper lining paper)
Masking tape
Newspaper
Sheet of plastic
Scissors
Pencil
Blu-tack
Paint
Paintbrushes
Ruler

1 Tape the paper to a rigid surface, preferably a wall, using masking tape.

2 Cover the floor in front of the wall with newspaper or a sheet of plastic.

3 Paint any large background areas first. For example, if you are attempting a beach scene then start at the top of your paper by painting the sky using a light blue, then progress down the paper using a dark blue for the sea and finally yellow for the sand. This last area should be the largest starting, approximately half-way down the paper and finishing at the bottom.

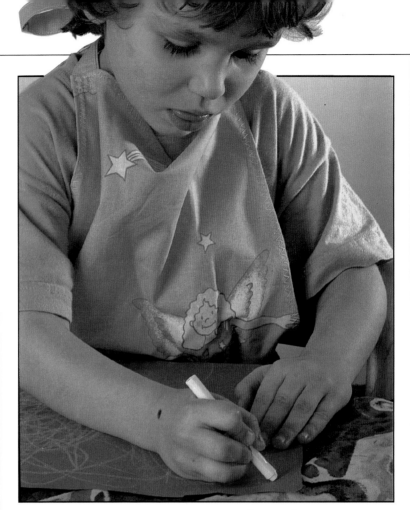

4 Clouds can be added to the sky area by painting directly onto the pale blue once it has dried.

5 Cut out newspaper shapes representing objects you wish to appear on your backdrop such as buckets, spades, sandcastles, flags, rocks, shells, boats, etc. Ensure they are large enough to be seen from a distance.

6 Place all the objects on the background with Blu-tack or masking tape. Move them around until you are satisfied with the positioning.

7 Draw around each object using the pencil and then remove from the wall.

8 Paint inside the line you have drawn or, alternatively, draw round your shape onto plain paper, paint and replace it on the wall to give a three-dimensional look.

Wax Resist Painting

This is an easy way for very young children to create effective paintings which look attractive on the wall.

YOU WILL NEED
Newspaper
Plain paper
Wax crayons
Watered-down paint
Thick paintbrushes

1 Cover your work surface with newspaper.

2 Place paper on this and draw a pattern on it with wax crayons. Use heavy,

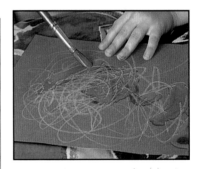

bold lines as they will create more effective patterns.

3 Select a paint and cover all the paper with this one colour. Allow to dry. The areas covered with wax will resist the paint and stand out from the background colour.

CHAPTER TWO
MODELLING

This section uses a variety of materials including clay, papier mâché, Fimo, marzipan and plaster of Paris. Always read the instructions carefully before starting a project and have everything near to hand. Plaster of Paris, for example, sets quickly and so it must be poured into the mould fast and the container you mixed it in must be wiped out with paper as quickly as you can. Do not pour wet plaster of Paris down a drain or sink as it will become blocked. Put unused clay back into a plastic bag to keep it moist and keep Fimo wrapped up. When making papier mâché leave it to dry between layers.

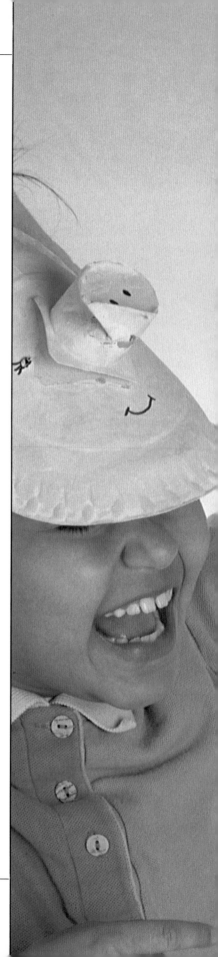

Modelling with Fimo

Fimo is a wonderfully versatile modelling material that comes in a variety of colours. It can be moulded, carved, marbled, varnished and baked in an oven.

Before working with Fimo you have to knead it to make it soft and pliable. The heat from your hands should do this. Just put a ball of Fimo in your hands and squeeze it. You can then roll out the Fimo with a rolling pin the same way that you roll out pastry. Cut out and shape pieces to form leaves or flowers, or use it to make different-shaped buttons. For example, try making geometric ones with triangular, square, rectangular, star or diamond shaped pieces of Fimo.

You can obtain an attractive marbled effect by kneading two or more colours of Fimo together.

It can be hardened by baking in an oven which should be preheated to 140°C (275°F) or Gas mark 1. Place the Fimo object on a baking tray covered with aluminium foil. Bake it for 15 to 20 minutes, depending on

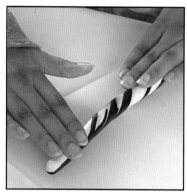

Knead together different colours to create a marbled effect.

the size of the object. Check the Fimo does not overcook as it will go brown.

You can buy a special laquer to spray over your finished object to give it a shiny protective coat. Clear nail varnish can also be used as an effective alternative.

Fimo can also be used to make a mould. This is particularly useful when you want to make a series of shapes that are all the same size, for example, buttons. The object you wish to copy should have a raised surface (a coin is a good object to use). Roll out a piece of Fimo and press the object into it. Lift off the Fimo which will contain an impression of the object. Place the Fimo on a baking tray and bake

until it is hard and you have your mould.

To make copies of the original object, simply press Fimo into the mould and then lift out the Fimo shape, trimming if necessary.

Fridge Magnets

Fridge magnets make good gifts and are also very useful.

YOU WILL NEED
Fimo
Poster paint
Paintbrush
Clear nail varnish
Small round magnet
A strong glue such as Bostik

1 Knead the Fimo for a few minutes until it is soft.

2 Roll out the Fimo and cut out or model the desired shape.

3 Bake it in the oven (*see left*).

4 Once it has cooled, paint it with poster paint and allow the shape to dry.

5 Coat the shape with a layer of clear varnish.

6 Glue the magnet to the back of the shape.

Fimo Jewellery

Jewellery made from Fimo looks attractive and can be made by all ages. See 'Modelling with Fimo' opposite for general instructions on how to use Fimo. You can either buy jewellery findings such as brooch backs, links and clasps or simply make holes in the beads and use shirring elastic.

YOU WILL NEED

Fimo – various colours
Rolling pin
Board on which to roll Fimo
Raw spaghetti, cocktail sticks or a knitting needle
Lump of plasticine
Aluminium foil
Baking tray
Paints
Thread or leather thong

Long Beads
1 Preheat the oven to 140°C (275°F), Gas mark 1.

2 Select a colour and break off a large piece of Fimo.

3 Knead the Fimo until it is warm and pliable.

4 Roll out some long pieces on the board and cut into lengths of equal size.

5 Make holes in each piece with a piece of spaghetti or a cocktail stick. If larger holes are needed use a knitting needle.

6 Place the beads on a baking tray covered with aluminium foil.

7 Place in the preheated oven for 15 to 20 minutes until it is hard. Check they do not overcook as they will go brown.

8 Decorate the beads with paint when cool.

9 Use the thread or leather thong to string the beads.

Round Beads
1 Follow steps 1–3 for long beads.

2 Cut pieces of equal size and roll each into a ball.

3 Make a hole through each bead with a needle.

4 Follow steps 6–9 for long beads.

Square Beads
1 Follow steps 1–3 for long beads.

2 Roll out a long piece of Fimo on the board and make it into a coil.

3 Flatten the coil with a piece of wood, so that it is square in section.

4 Cut the block into cubes or oblongs of the same size and make holes through the centre with a needle.

5 Follow steps 6–9 for long beads.

Tubular Beads

1 Follow steps 1–3 for long beads (*see page 25*).

2 Roll the Fimo out flat on the board.

3 Wrap it around a cylindrical object such as a knitting needle or pencil making sure the edges overlap.

4 Remove the knitting needle or pencil and cut the tube into pieces to make individual beads.

5 Follow steps 6–9 for long beads (*see page 25*).

Coin-Shaped Beads and Pendants

1 Follow steps 1–3 for long beads (*see page 25*).

2 Break off similar sized pieces of Fimo and roll into small balls.

3 Flatten each ball with a rolling pin.

4 Make holes in the centre if you want to make small beads or near the top if you want to make pendants.

5 Decorate the beads or pendants with different patterns and textures.

6 Follow steps 6–9 for long beads (*see page 25*).

Fimo Baby Brooch

YOU WILL NEED
Pink Fimo and one other colour
Glue
Brooch pin
Pencil
Aluminium foil
Baking tray

1 Preheat the oven to 140°C (275°F), Gas mark 1.

2 Roll out a small ball of pink Fimo for the head.

3 Press the point of the pencil into the Fimo to make the eyes and mouth.

4 Make the baby's nose from a tiny ball of pink Fimo and position it on the face.

5 Make the body from a pink sausage-shaped piece of Fimo and mould it onto the head.

6 Roll out a piece of Fimo using the other colour and wrap it around the baby as a blanket.

7 Place it on the baking tray covered with foil and cook in the oven until it is set hard. Remove and leave to cool.

8 Finally, glue the brooch pin onto the back.

26

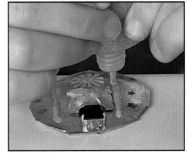

5 Decorate the shape by glueing on sequins and diamanté beads *(above)*.

6 Cut a piece of ribbon or material 20cm (8in) long.

7 Decorate the material with felt-tip pens.

8 Fold the ribbon in half and glue the raw ends to the back of the medal. Thread the safety pin through the fold and pin it to your jumper.

Paper Medals

YOU WILL NEED
Card
Scissors
Felt-tip pens
Gold-coloured foil
Sequins and diamanté beads
Glue
Striped ribbon or material you can colour with felt-tip pens
Large safety pin

1 Cut out a circle of card approximately 5cm (2in) in diameter.

2 Draw round the card circle on the back of the foil wrapping paper. Draw a

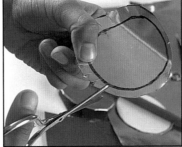

larger circle around the outside and cut it out.

3 Make a series of even cuts from the outer to the inner circle *(above)*.

4 Cover the card circle with the wrapping paper, taking care to glue all the cut edges down carefully so that all the card is covered *(top right)*.

27

Paper Beads

This is an easy and cheap way to make beads and different looks can be achieved by using old birthday and Christmas cards, wrapping paper, magazines and even newspaper.

YOU WILL NEED
Plain paper, card or coloured foil
Pencil
Ruler
Scissors
Glue
Plasticine
Poster paints
Paintbrushes
Clear nail varnish

1 Make a template from some card in the shape of an elongated triangle.

2 Draw around the template on the paper.

3 If you are using plain paper you can paint the triangles at this stage if you wish.

4 Cut the triangles out (*top right*).

5 Roll them round the pencil starting at the base (*below right*).

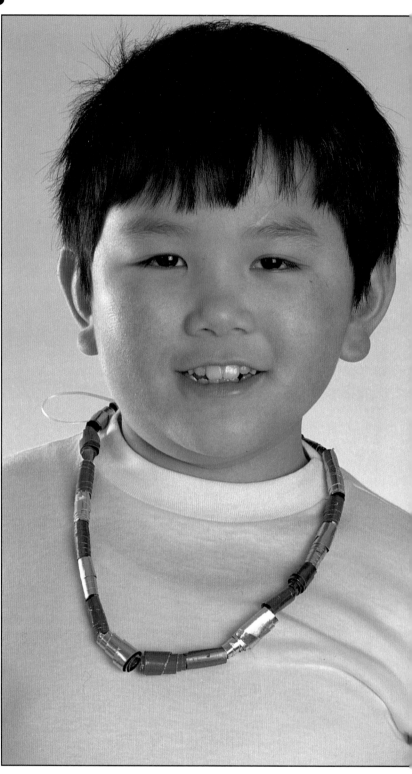

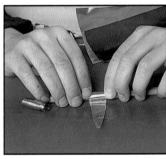

6 Glue the narrow end into position to keep the bead's shape.

7 When you have made a number of beads thread them back onto the pencil.

8 Stick the end of the pencil into the lump of plasticine and paint the beads. If you already painted the beads (*see step 3*) then you can leave them or give them another coat.

9 Paint the beads with clear nail varnish.

Papier Mâché Pulp

This is a very quick method of making a pulp which can then be used in the same way as you would use clay.

YOU WILL NEED
Large microwave-proof bowl
Newspaper – torn into small pieces
3 handfuls of plain flour
Water
Clingfilm

1 Place the newspaper in the bowl and cover with water.

2 Cover the bowl with clingfilm and prick a few holes in the surface using a fork or leave a small gap at the side to allow the steam to escape.

3 Place bowl in microwave and cook for five minutes.

4 Remove bowl, stir the mixture and return to the microwave for another five minutes.

5 Remove the bowl and stir in the flour.

6 Replace clingfilm ensuring the holes are still open or leave a gap at the side.

7 Return to microwave for three minutes.

8 Strain the mixture through an old pair of tights. The resulting grey pulpy mass is now ready to use as a modelling medium.

Papier Mâché

Papier mâché is easy to make and you can achieve sophisticated results for very little cost.

YOU WILL NEED
Newspaper
Wallpaper paste
Balloon or wire mesh or plastic container
Bowl

1 Make up the wallpaper paste in the bowl according to the instructions given.

2 Tear the newspaper into similar-sized strips.

3 Decide what you are going to use as a base to mould the papier mâché around. You could use a blown up balloon to make a bowl (*see page 31*); some wire mesh moulded into a bracelet shape for an attractive bangle; or moulded plasticine to make a puppet's head; or a plastic milk container to make a cat (*see page 30*).

4 Dip one of the newspaper strips into the paste, making sure it is covered completely in paste and stick it on the surface of your base shape. Repeat this process until the base is completely covered. Leave to dry overnight.

5 On the following day cover the original layer of paper with another layer and again allow it to dry overnight. Repeat until object is covered with seven or eight layers.

Papier Mâché Cat

YOU WILL NEED

Empty large plastic milk container
Sand or Gravel
A ball of rolled up newspaper for the cat's head
Newspaper
Wallpaper paste
Bowl
Card
Scissors
Masking tape
White emulsion paint
Poster or acrylic paint
Paintbrushes
Clear varnish

1 Clean out the empty milk container and fill it with sand or gravel to stop it falling over.

2 Remove lid from milk container and push ball of rolled up newspaper into neck. Secure it with masking tape (*see right*).

3 Follow the instructions for Papier Mâché on page 29 until you have four complete layers.

4 Make the ears by cutting two triangles from the card. Bend them in the middle and tape them onto the head.

Papier Mâché Bowl

5 Cover the entire model (including the ears) with another three layers of papier mâché. Remember to allow each layer to dry thoroughly.

6 Paint the model with white emulsion paint and leave to dry

7 Paint the cat with acrylic or poster paint. Use whatever colours you like – it doesn't have to be a 'real' cat colour.

8 Coat with clear varnish.

Alternatives

● Make an angel by sticking a large triangle of card onto the back of the container (*see below*) instead of ears. Decorate with paint and tinsel.

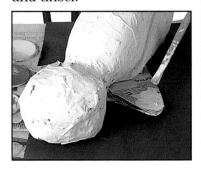

YOU WILL NEED
Balloon
Cotton
Newspaper
Wallpaper paste
Bowl
Card
Scissors
White emulsion paint
Paintbrushes
Poster or acrylic paint
Clear varnish

1 Blow up a round balloon, knot it and tie a piece of thread round the knot.

2 Tear the newspaper into similar-sized strips.

3 Mix the wallpaper paste in the bowl, according to the instructions given on the packet.

4 Dip one of the newspaper strips into the paste, completely covering it with paste, wrap it around the balloon making sure it is smoothed down. Repeat this process until three-quarters of the balloon's surface has been covered.

5 Hang the balloon in a doorway overnight to dry.

6 Cover the same half of the balloon with another layer of newspaper and again leave to dry. Repeat this process until the balloon has been covered with seven or eight layers.

7 When completely dry, pop the balloon and remove it gently from the newspaper bowl.

8 If you want to make a rim for the bowl then tape a strip of card about 12mm (½in) in width to the edge of the existing papier mâché. Cover this with two or three more layers of papier mâché.

9 When completely dry paint the inside and outside of the bowl with white emulsion.

10 Allow to dry and decorate the bowl using acrylic or poster paint.

11 When the paint has dried cover the surface with clear varnish to give a protective finish.

Salt Dough

This is a very good substitute for clay and can be used to make models, Christmas tree decorations, or picture frames.

YOU WILL NEED
3 cups plain flour
1 cup salt
1 tsp glycerine (this is not essential but it makes the dough a lot easier to work with – buy it from the chemist)
1 cup of water
sieve

Note: The size of the cup is not important as long as the same cup is used for each measurement.

1 Sieve the dry ingredients into a bowl and add the glycerine.

2 Pour in the water stirring continuously.

3 Continue stirring until the mixture is fairly stiff.

4 Knead the mixture together. If it is too dry, add more water and if it is too wet, add more flour. (If you do not wish to use the dough immediately, wrap it up in clingfilm or place in an airtight plastic container and store in a cool place for a few days.)

Salt Dough Garlands

YOU WILL NEED
Salt dough (*see left*)
Tea plate
Knife
Paperclip
Baking tray
Poster paint
Paintbrushes

1 Preheat oven to 180°C (350°F) or Gas mark 4.

2 Roll out two sausage shaped rolls of dough about the width of two fingers.

3 Place the tea plate upside down on the baking tray and twist together the rolls of dough round the edge of the plate.

4 Join the ends together and remove the plate.

5 Roll out some more dough and cut out diamond shapes to make some leaves. Score with a knife to indicate the veins.

6 Make berries from tiny balls of dough and use a skewer to make indentations at the top of each ball.

7 Press the leaves and berries into the circle of twisted dough at intervals to create clusters of foliage.

8 You can also make a fruit garland by modelling apple, pear and banana shapes which are then placed on the twists of dough.

9 Press the paperclip into the back of the garland near the top so it is slightly proud at one end.

10 Bake it in the oven until hard.

11 Paint the garland once it has cooled.

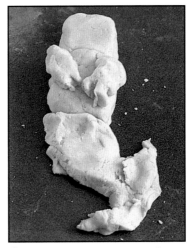

2 Using larger pieces of dough, model her body, arms and tail. Make sure you press the sections together so they do not split apart when baked.

3 Squeeze some salt dough through the garlic press and place the resulting strands on the head to make the hair.

4 Using the point of a pencil make holes for the eyes and mouth. Use a tiny piece of dough to make the nose and add textures to the tail for fish scales.

5 Place in a preheated oven at 180°C (350°F) or Gas mark 4 and bake until hard.

6 Once the dough has cooled, decorate the mermaid with paint.

Salt Dough Mermaid

YOU WILL NEED
Salt dough (*see opposite*)
Garlic press
Baking tray
Poster paint
Paintbrushes

1 Roll out a small ball of salt dough for the mermaid's head and place on the baking tray.

Salt Dough Name Plaques

YOU WILL NEED
Salt dough (*see page 32*)
Card
Pencil
Scissors
Rolling pin
Knife
Paperclip
Baking tray
Poster Paint
Paintbrushes

1 Preheat the oven to 180°C (350°F) or Gas mark 4.

2 Cut out an oval template from the card.

3 Roll out the dough.

4 Place the template on the dough and cut around it.

5 Roll out thin sausages of dough about the width of a pencil.

6 Using these thin rolls of dough, form the letters of the name you wish to put

on the plaque and place them on the oval of dough.

7 Press the paperclip into the back of the plaque so it is slightly proud at one end.

8 Bake in the preheated oven until the dough is hard.

9 Once the dough has cooled, decorate the plaque with paint.

Plaster-of-Paris Ring Stand

YOU WILL NEED
Plaster of Paris
Water
Rubber glove
Paint
Paintbrushes
Clear nail varnish

1 Mix together the plaster of Paris with water as instructed on the packet.

2 Carefully fill the glove with the plaster checking that the mixture reaches the tips of the fingers.

3 Hang it up to dry.

4 When the plaster has set gently peel off the glove.

5 Paint the plaster hand and coat it with clear nail varnish if you want a shiny finish.

Plaster Shells

YOU WILL NEED
Clay
Plaster of Paris
Rolling pin
Shells
Paints
Paintbrush

1 Roll out the clay to the size and shape you wish the finished picture to be.

2 Press a shell firmly into the clay so it leaves an imprint when removed. Repeat the process using the same or different shells.

3 Roll out a sausage shape with another piece of clay and make a wall around the perimeter of the base. Make sure the join is properly sealed.

4 Mix the plaster of Paris according to the instructions on the packet and pour this over the clay.

5 Allow it to set and, when hard enough, carefully remove the clay.

6 This can then be painted or left as it is.

Plaster Casting Hands and Feet

This is fun and a lovely keepsake especially of young childrens' hands and feet.

YOU WILL NEED
Clay
Rolling pin
Plaster of Paris
Paints
Paintbrush

1 Roll out a piece of clay larger than your hand.

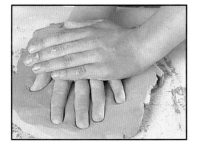

2 Press the back of your hand into the clay so it leaves an impression when removed.

3 Build up a small wall of clay around the edge of the hand-imprinted clay.

4 Make sure the join between the wall and the flat surface of the clay is very tight. Add more clay if necessary.

5 Mix the plaster according to the instructions given on the packet.

6 Pour it over the clay mould. Leave it to set.

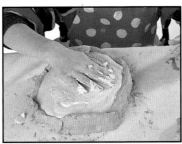

7 When it is hard, carefully remove the clay and you will be left with a plaster replica of your fingers.

8 You can either paint the cast or leave it as it is.

9 Make a cast of your foot using exactly the same method. Simply press your foot into the clay instead of your hand.

Marzipan Fruits

Real marzipan is made from ground almonds and is delicious. It tastes nothing like shop-bought marzipan so it is worth making yourself, if you have the time.

YOU WILL NEED
100g (4oz) finely ground almonds
100g (4 oz) icing sugar
1 egg white
Red, blue, yellow and green food colouring
Cloves

Equipment
Bowl
Clean, dry cloth
Fine paintbrushes
Saucer
Paper cases for sweets
Box

1 Mix together the almonds, sifted icing sugar and egg white.

2 Remove from the bowl and knead the mixture together until it becomes a smooth dry paste.

3 Roll the paste into a ball, cover it with a cloth and leave it to stand for 15 minutes.

4 Split the marzipan into walnut size pieces and roll them into the fruit shapes you want such as bananas, oranges, melons, apples, grapes or pears.

5 Paint the fruit with food colouring and combine colours if necessary, for example, yellow and red food colouring together to make orange, and for green, mix blue and yellow.

6 Stick cloves into the oranges, apples and pears to form stems.

7 Place the marzipan fruits in little paper cases and put them in an attractive box (*see Découpage, page 49*) to make a lovely present.

Marzipan Monsters

These are fun to make and model and are delightful gifts.

YOU WILL NEED
Marzipan (*see left*)
Food colouring
Whole almonds
Chocolate strands and chocolate drops
Vermicelli
Edible silver balls
Red liquorice
Narrow paintbrush

1 Break off a piece of marzipan and roll it into a ball about the size of a cherry. This will be the head of the monster.

2 Break off another large piece of marzipan and make an oval shape for the body tapering it at one end to represent the tail.

3 Join these two shapes together and paint with food colouring.

4 Place whole almonds down the 'spine' of the monster right to the tip of the tail.

5 Place silver balls in the head to represent the eyes.

6 Use the red liquorice to make the tongue.

7 Use the chocolate strands and drops, and vermicelli to add further decoration.

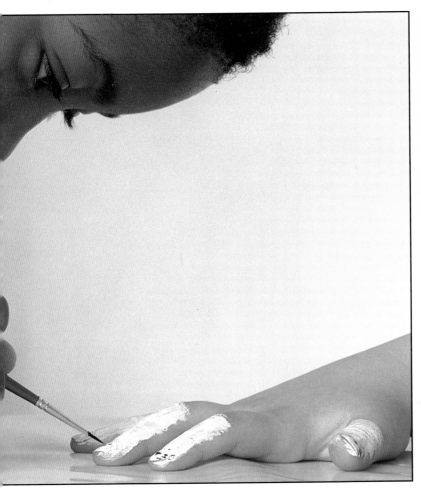

Real Finger Puppets

Mention finger puppets and people think of fingers with a felt cover, but there is an alternative – real finger puppets.

YOU WILL NEED
Ball-point pens
Felt-tip pens
Crayons
Powder paint
Water
Paper
Pencil

1 Place your hand on a piece of paper and draw around it. Use this to work out a design.

2 Wash and dry your hand so that it is clean.

3 Skin absorbs colour so it is a good idea to paint your fingers white to start with so the colours stand out.

4 Paint or draw the outline first and then fill in with colour.

Finger Mice

1 Paint fingers white from the middle knuckles to the fingertips.

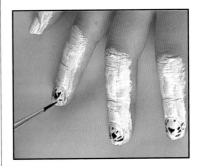

2 Draw two eyes, a mouth and some whiskers on each fingernail.

3 Above each fingernail draw two circles of pink to represent the ears.

4 In the middle of each finger, from the first joint extending as far as the second or further, draw a tail in the same colour as the rest of the body. You now have five mice at the tips of your fingers.

Paper Plate Masks

You can very easily make a great variety of masks using paper plates.

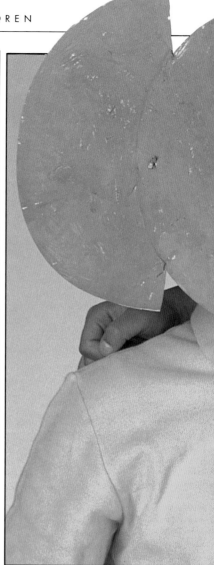

YOU WILL NEED

One paper plate for each mask
Pencil
Scissors
Shirring elastic and needle
Paper or thin card for ears etc.
Masking tape
Egg boxes for noses
Wool or string for hair and whiskers
Glue or staples
Paint or felt-tip pens
Kitchen roll tube (for the elephant mask)
Pink felt and empty fromage frais container (for the pig mask)

1 Work out a design on paper.

2 Hold a plate up to your face very carefully and mark the position of your eyes. Cut out two small holes using the scissors.

3 Pierce a hole at either side of the plate, parallel with the eye marks about 2cm (¾in) in from the edge.

4 Tie the elastic through one hole. Hold the plate up to your face to check how much you need to go round your head.

5 Tie the other end of elastic through the opposite hole so that the mask sits comfortably but securely in position.

6 Cut out noses, hair, ears, whiskers, etc. and glue these into place.

7 Cut away the lower part of the mask if you wish to add fangs for frightening animals.

Elephant Mask

1 Follow steps 1–5 for Paper Plate Masks (*see left*).

2 Tape the kitchen roll tube to the plate for the elephant's trunk. Cut half-way round the tube, about 12cm (5in) above the plate, to enable the trunk to bend.

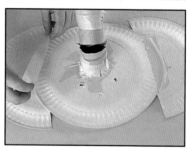

3 Cut out two large elephant ears from card, or cut a paper plate in half, and tape them to the plate.

4 Paint the whole thing grey and allow to dry.

Pig Mask

1 Follow steps 1–5 for Paper Plate Masks (*see opposite*).

2 Squash a fromage frais container, paint it pink and glue it onto the plate for the pig's nose. (Mix the paint with PVA glue so that it sticks to the container).

3 Cut out ears from pink felt and glue them into place.

4 Paint the plate pink.

5 Draw a mouth with a felt-tip pen.

Rabbit or Cat Mask

1 Follow steps 1–5 for Paper Plate Masks (*see opposite*).

2 Cut out long rabbit- or cat-shaped ears and whiskers from some card.

3 Paint the eyeholes and draw in a nose.

4 Stick on the whiskers and ears.

CHAPTER THREE

CRAFTING

As with all craft projects, especially those using dyes, paints, inks and water, cover your work area with newspaper or decorator's plastic sheeting. Some of the skills needed in this section, such as sewing, take time to learn and are not suitable for very young children. Patchwork can be simple if worked in oblongs or squares, or it can be quite complicated if using more complex ideas, such as the log cabin design. It is fun to use fabrics from old clothes and old curtains so that the patchwork becomes an heirloom. Recycle odd socks to make sock puppets. Try making a range of characters such as a snake, a dragon and a dog, and make up your own play.

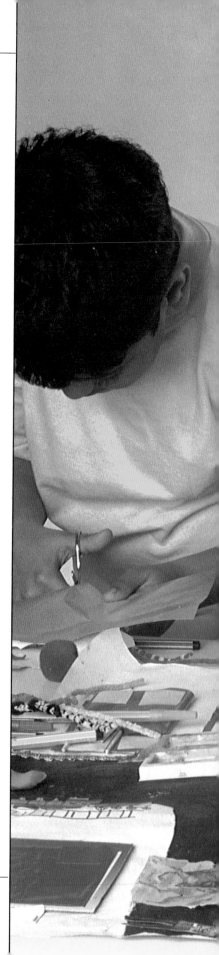

Microwave Tie Dye

This is an exceedingly fast method to tie dye clothes and does away with all the time needed for soaking.

YOU WILL NEED
Garment or cloth for tie dying
Dylon dye produced especially for this purpose
Receptacle in which to dye the material

1 Follow the instructions on the Dylon dye container. You will achieve a tie dyed, scrunched, twisted or folded effect with any garment.

Traditional Tie Dyeing

This is an ancient technique which we still use to decorate fabric. There are never any two designs which are the same so you will always have a unique garment.

Tights

YOU WILL NEED
Light coloured pair of tights
Dylon powder dye
Dylon cold dye fix
Measuring jug
Salt
Water
Wooden spoon
Bucket of cold water

1 Wash the tights.

2 Tie a series of knots in both legs of the tights.

3 Mix the dye in the measuring jug following the instructions on the pack.

4 Mix four heaped tablespoonfuls of salt with the cold dye fix for each tin of dye used.

5 Pour the cold dye fix into the bucket of cold water and add the dye solution. Mix it well with the wooden spoon.

6 Add the wet tights and stir continuously for ten minutes making sure they are totally submerged. Leave for a further 50 minutes stirring occasionally.

7 Remove the tights, rinse them and leave them to dry.

8 Untie the knots to reveal the pattern.

Tie-Dye T-Shirt

YOU WILL NEED
Light coloured plain T-shirt
Cotton
Dylon powder dye
Dylon cold dye fix
Measuring jug
Water
Salt
Bucket
Wooden Spoon
Ironing Board
Iron

1 Wash the T-shirt.

2 Draw up small clumps of fabric and tie securely and tightly with cotton. Repeat this process all over the T-shirt.

3 Mix the dye and the cold dye fix pouring in a bucket of cold water as before. (*See steps 3–5 for Traditional Tie Dyeing*).

4 Repeat steps 6 and 7 for Traditional Tie Dyeing.

5 Untie the cotton and the pattern will be revealed.

6 Iron the T-shirt.

Collages

A collage is a collection of bits and pieces of paper put together in a pleasing manner to form either a decorative or representational image.

Ripped Paper Collage

YOU WILL NEED
Selection of papers (newspaper, magazines, stamps, wrapping paper, bits of corrugated card, tissue, crepe and coloured papers)
Thin card on which to make the collage
Glue
Scissors (optional)

1 Rip the paper into different sized pieces and lay them out on the card.

2 When you are satisfied with the arrangement glue the pieces, either partly or wholly, to the card.

3 Paper can be ripped in different ways so if you wish to form a bird, for example, rip the paper into tiny bits and glue only the ends of the pieces thus making the paper stand away from the card to give a feathery appearance.

Three-Dimensional Collage

YOU WILL NEED
Household waste (empty boxes and cartons, toilet rolls, netting from bags of fruit, milk bottle tops, empty tubes, etc.)
Card on which to build the collage
Glue
Scissors (optional)

1 Study the material you have available and place it on the card.

2 Glue the pieces into place ensuring you apply enough glue as the items may be relatively heavy.

Souvenir Collage

YOU WILL NEED
Postcards
Bus or train tickets
Receipts
Glue
Paper or thin card on which to make the picture

1 Place the card on a flat surface and lay out all the souvenirs.

2 Lay the souvenirs out on the paper and move them around until you are satisfied with their layout.

3 Glue the pieces down either wholly or partly and allow some to overlap others.

Decorate A Duvet

This is a great way to brighten up a bedroom and is a fun though time-consuming task.

YOU WILL NEED
Old plain, light-coloured duvet cover and or a pillow case
Paper
Pencil
Set of fabric pens
Newspaper
Bin Bag
Iron
Ironing board

1 Work out a design on the piece of paper first and decide upon the colours you wish to use.

2 Draw the design on the fabric in pencil before you start using the pens.

3 Cover any surface you are working on with newspaper and place a few layers, or bin bags, inside the cover to stop any colours bleeding through.

4 Now use the pens to outline or shade any large areas of colour in your design.

5 When finished, turn the duvet inside out and iron on the back to fix the colours.

6 Repeat the same process for the pillow case and make a matching set.

Making a Dried-Flower Press

A flower press is a useful object to have in case you wish to preserve any flowers. The dried flowers do not have to be used immediately but will keep until they are needed.

YOU WILL NEED
Two pieces of plywood 20 × 20cm (8 × 8in)
Hand drill
Four large butterfly nuts and screws
Sheets of corrugated card or cardboard
Sheets of blotting paper
Pencil

1 Draw a cross just inside the corners of each piece of plywood. Drill a hole through each of the marked crosses.

2 Push the screws through the holes on one of the plywood boards.

3 Cut the cardboard and paper into squares that will fit inside the screws.

4 Remove the screws and lie one piece of card on top of the board followed by two pieces of blotting paper. Repeat this process until all the card and paper has been used up.

5 Now place the other plywood board on top and push the screws through both boards and secure with the wing nuts.

6 To press flowers, grasses or leaves, unscrew the wing nuts, remove the top board and place the specimens between the sheets of blotting paper.

7 Replace the top board, screw the nuts back again as tightly as possible and leave for about a week.

8 Remove the dried specimens and use in whatever way you wish, for example you could glue them to stiff paper to make greetings cards.

Card Making

Homemade cards are always appreciated and are very easy to make, so why not have a go.

General Hints
1 Choose an envelope first so that you can decide on the card size before starting to make it.

2 When folding a card always fold exactly. Use a ruler to give a sharp line.

3 Always remember to allow any writing inside a folded card to dry before designing the front otherwise it will smudge.

4 Write any words lightly so that you can space the lettering correctly and rub it out when finished.

Stained Glass Christmas Card

YOU WILL NEED
Black card approximately
21 × 15cm (8 × 6in)
Tissue paper
Pencil
Scissors
Glue
Envelope for the finished card

1 Fold the card in half.

2 Draw a design on one side of the folded card and cut around the shape or

shapes. Remember – the simpler the design the easier it will be to cut out.

3 Lay a piece of tissue over the cutout and trace a larger version of the shape onto the tissue paper *(see right)*.

4 Dab some glue on the back of the card and stick down the tissue paper. Leave it to dry.

Valentine Card

YOU WILL NEED
Piece of white card
Red tissue paper
Pictures of cherubs or flowers
(cut from magazines)
Copydex glue

1 Carefully fold the white card in half.

2 Stick the cherub picture in the centre front of the white card.

3 Cut out tiny red hearts from the tissue paper and stick round the cherub.

4 Alternatively, cut out a heart from plain paper and decorate with a doily or lace edge.

5 Different coloured tissue paper can be used to cover the cutout to make it look like real stained glass, but this takes more time and skill.

47

Sewn Birthday Card

YOU WILL NEED
Shiny card
Thread
Darning needle
Pencil
Glue

1 Cut out two pieces of card each measuring 21×30cm (8×12in).

2 Thread the needle and tie a knot at the end of it.

3 Fold both pieces of card in half.

4 Write 'HAPPY BIRTHDAY' in capital letters on the front of one of the pieces of card.

5 Beginning from the back of the card, sew around the words you have written.

6 Glue the second piece of card onto the inside of the first so that the thread and knot are covered.

Pop-up Card

YOU WILL NEED
Two pieces of thin card approximately 21×21cm (8×8in)
Pencil
Ruler
Scissors
Felt-tip pens

1 Fold one piece of card in half. Crease along the fold.

2 Use a pencil and ruler to draw two horizontal parallel lines 6cm (2½in) apart from the centre fold to almost half way across the card (*see right*).

3 Cut along these lines.

4 Fold back the section that you have just cut and crease along the dotted line. (*see far right*).

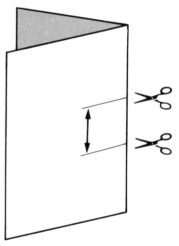

Decorated Boxes (Découpage)

Découpage is the art of sticking paper onto surfaces as a form of decoration. It is an easy way of creating an interesting decorative finish without having to be a talented artist and can be applied to small items such as boxes, cartons, calendars and greeting cards.

YOU WILL NEED
Box or carton (old shoe boxes or cereal boxes are ideal)
Bits of brightly coloured paper (cut out from old magazines)
Glue
Scissors
Poster paint
Paintbrushes
Varnish or sticky-backed plastic

1 Paint the box and leave it to dry.

2 If any lettering shows through, give it another coat of paint.

3 Cut out some simple shapes from the coloured paper.

4 Glue the shapes onto the box.

5 Cover the box with a coat of clear varnish for protection.

5 Open out the card and push out the centre.

6 Design and colour the front of the card and turn the pop-up sections into faces, animals or houses.

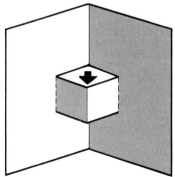

7 You can cut out another pop-out section from the first pop-up.

8 Glue this finished card onto the other card.

Leopard Box

YOU WILL NEED
Plastic box with a hinged lid
(an empty box of baby wipes
is ideal)
Newspaper
Card
Masking tape
Poster paints (white, yellow,
black and pink)

1 Measure out an oblong piece of card the same width as the back of the box but about twice the height. Using the diagram below as a guide, draw a pencil outline of this shape onto the card and cut out. These are the leopard's ears. Tape the shaped card onto the back of the box using masking tape.

2 Measure out another piece of card the same width and about half the height of the front of the box. Round of the corners and cut a small triagular shape for the mouth (*see right*). Tape the card to the front of the box.

3 Cut out a heart shape without the point for the nose. Tape in place.

4 Cover the whole box with four layers of papier

mâché (*see page 29*). If you wish to paint the inside of the box, cover with one layer of papier mâché.

5 Cut out eight elongated triangles from some card and tape them onto the inside of the lid; four on

each side. Cover with papier mâché. These are the leopard's teeth.

6 Paint the whole thing white – you may need to use several layers to completely cover the newsprint.

7 Cover with a base coat of yellow. Draw in the leopard's paws, eyes, and ears with a pencil and paint the appropriate colour (*see above*). Finally paint in the leopard's black spots and leave to dry.

Stamp Decorated Box

YOU WILL NEED
Same as for Découpage
(*see page 49*)
Substitute stamps for brightly
coloured paper

1 Collect old stamps from letters.

2 Glue them to the box you have chosen to decorate making sure they overlap.

3 Cover with either clear sticky-backed plastic or a coat of varnish.

Dried Flower Boxes

YOU WILL NEED
Same as for Découpage
(*see page 49*)
Substitute dried flowers for brightly
coloured paper
Copydex
Tweezers

1 To dry flowers see Making a Dried-Flower press on page 45.

2 Paint the box with poster paint and leave to dry.

3 Give the box another coat if any lettering still shows through.

4 Place a layer of copydex on the areas you wish to stick the flowers.

5 Gently lift the flowers with a pair of tweezers and place them onto the glued areas.

Sweet Covered Boxes

YOU WILL NEED
Same as for Découpage
(*see page 49*)
Substitute miniature sweets such as
dolly mixtures or jelly babies for
brightly coloured paper
PVA glue

1 Buy miniature sweets and leave them to dry in an airing cupboard for a week.

2 Glue them onto the top of the box.

3 Paint the box with a layer of varnish made from a 50/50 mixture of PVA glue and water.

Skittles

YOU WILL NEED
10 empty plastic drink bottles
Ball
Funnel
Filling (dried peas, beans or rice)
Newspaper
Wallpaper paste
Poster or, acrylic paints
Paintbrushes
Clear varnish

1 Clean the bottles, inside and out. Leave to dry.

2 Remove caps and use the funnel to pour in the filling.

3 Test the filled bottles to see if they fall down when hit with the ball. If they don't, take some of the filling out and try again.

4 Mix the wallpaper paste according to the instructions on the packet.

5 Rip the newspaper into strips and cover with paste. Stick them to the bottles overlapping the pieces until the whole bottle is covered.

6 Leave to dry overnight. Repeat stage 5, five times.

7 When all the bottles have been covered with six layers of paper and are completely dry, paint them with white paint. If newsprint shows through apply another coat.

8 Decorate the bottles with bright colours.

9 Varnish bottles to protect them and leave to dry.

Puffy Paint Gym Shoes

Puffy paint expands upon heating so when using on fabric the design you create will stand out from the material.

YOU WILL NEED
Use old plimsolls or any cheap
canvas shoes such as espadrilles
Pencil
Piece of paper
Newspaper
Puffy fabric paints

1 Draw a design on a piece of paper so that you know exactly what you are doing before you begin.

2 Stuff the shoe with newspaper.

3 Using a pencil, lightly draw your design onto the canvas.

4 Now use the puffy pens to colour your pattern taking care not to touch areas you wish to leave plain and ensuring you do not let one colour run into another.

5 Place the finished shoes in an airing cupboard as heat is needed to create the puffy look of the paint.

6 Change laces (if the shoes have them) for ribbons or dayglo laces if you want to completely alter the look of the old shoes.

Puffy Paint T-Shirt

YOU WILL NEED
Plain T-shirt
Pen
Piece of paper
Masking tape
Card
Puffy fabric paints
Iron
Ironing board

1 Work out your design on a piece of paper.

2 Stretch the T-shirt over some card to prevent the paint going through to the back.

3 Copy your design onto the T-shirt using the puffy paint.

4 Leave the paint to dry for 20 to 30 minutes.

5 Turn the T-shirt inside out and iron over the back of the design for 15 seconds. Make sure the iron is on the silk or wool setting. The warmth of the iron will fix the colours and make the paint puff up.

Alternatively, try using glitter paints or fabric pens instead of the puffy paint. Be aware that glitter paint will gradually come off with washing.

Buttons T-Shirt

A simple and cheap way to brighten up an old T-shirt or to make a plain white one more interesting.

YOU WILL NEED
Plain T-shirt
Selection of buttons
Pencil
Thread
Needle

1 Lightly pencil your name, or just your initials, onto the T-shirt to get the spacing correct.

2 Sew the buttons onto the pencilled letters. It may take quite a number of buttons but the effect is worth the effort.

53

Puffy Paint Hairband

YOU WILL NEED
Plain, fabric covered hairband
Puffy fabric paints (3 colours)

1 Draw a zigzag pattern down the centre of the hairband, taking care not to smudge the paint.

2 Using a different colour paint, make a series of dots down one side of the zigzag pattern and another colour to make dots down the other side.

Mosaics

This takes some time to complete but it is a very effective way of creating a picture. Mosaics were originally created using small stones of different colours but using areas of colour from old magazines or cards is just as interesting and easier.

YOU WILL NEED
Old magazines, cereal boxes, cards and wrapping paper
Scissors
Glue
Sheet of paper on which to do the mosaic
Empty yoghurt pots

1 Cut up the magazines, cereal boxes, cards and wrapping paper into small pieces about 1cm (½in) square.

2 Group the pieces together according to their colours and then divide each colour into different shades. Place the different shades in separate containers.

3 Work out a design on the piece of paper and decide on the areas of colour.

4 Glue the pieces to the paper and slowly build up the picture.

Face Painting – a Clown

Creating your own clown's face is fun though you will find it easier to paint someone else's face rather than your own. Real clowns have to register their make-up as an original design before they are allowed to use it but you can do this for free. You do not have to use expensive stage make-up but can try using your mother's old make-up.

YOU WILL NEED

Face paints or old make-up not used by your mother
Hair grips, slides, or a hairband

1 Pin your hair back or hold it off your face with a hairband.

2 Spread a light foundation cream all over your face.

3 Make an outline of a big mouth, much larger than your own, in brown or black make-up if you are fair-skinned and white if you are dark-skinned. If you want a happy face turn up the corners of the mouth

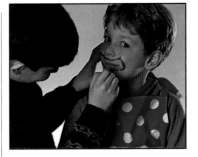

and for a sad face turn them down.

4 Fill in the mouth with a bright red.

5 Draw a large circle or a cross shape around the eyes which again contrasts with your face. Do not go too near the eyes them-selves. Fill in the outline with an unusual colour such as purple or pink.

6 Draw extended eyelashes in dark brown, black or blue. (An eye pencil is good for this).

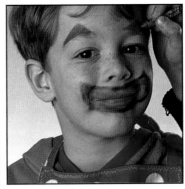

7 Make strangely shaped eyebrows.

8 Colour your nose red or stick on a red nose (like the ones you see on Red Nose Day).

9 If your clown is sad draw on tears.

Paper Hats

The instructions given here are for a magician's hat but simple additions and variations can produce a whole variety of paper hats very easily.

YOU WILL NEED
Dinner plate
Thin card or thick paper
Black, silver and gold poster paints
Paintbrush
Elastic
Glue (preferably Copydex)
Scissors
Paperclip

Optional
Tissue
Crepe paper
Tinsel
Pasta shapes
Beads

1 Put the plate face down on the card or paper and draw round it.

2 Draw a line across the centre of the circle and cut along it to make two semi-circles from which you can make two hats.

3 Paint one semicircle black and leave it to dry.

4 Then paint moons and stars in gold and silver onto this black background.

5 When the paint is dry, bring the two ends of the straight edge together to form a cone. Glue the edges together and hold in place with a paperclip and allow it to dry.

Felt Table Mats

A simple idea to make the table look attractive if someone is coming around.

YOU WILL NEED
Felt
Other fabric scraps
Fabric glue
Scissors
Felt-tip pen
Large dinner plates

1 Place the dinner plate face down onto a piece of felt and draw round it with the felt-tip pen.

2 Cut out the circle.

3 Cut out food shapes from the other scraps of fabric, for example, chips, eggs or tomatoes, and glue them onto the felt plate to make a food table mat. (Fawn-coloured towelling makes good fish fingers and small green felt circles make excellent peas).

and your thumb where the heel should be.

2 Bend your fingers and make a mark where the eyes should go.

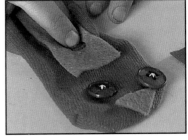

3 Use two coloured buttons for the eyes and sew them into place.

4 Cut out a long, narrow piece of felt and sew it into the mouth for the tongue.

5 Decorate the body with pieces of coloured felt and sequins.

Alternatives
● If you would prefer to make a seal, use a grey sock and sew black buttons on for the eyes and nose. Poke some pipe cleaners through the end of the sock for its whiskers.

6 Make two holes opposite one another, 1cm (½in) from the bottom of the cone. Thread the elastic through the holes feeding it through from the outside and securing it with a knot on the inside.

Alternatives
● Make a cone from the other semicircle of card and stick strips of crepe paper to the point of the hat to create a medieval head-dress.
● Paint the card green and glue tinsel and painted pasta bows to it to make a Christmas tree hat.
● Make a clown's hat, by painting the card in a bright colour and adding three pom-poms to the front.

Snake Sock Puppet

This is a good way to use those odd socks that every household seems to have!

YOU WILL NEED
Sock (preferably multicoloured)
Pieces of felt
Buttons
Sequins
Fabric glue
Needle
Thread

1 Place the sock on your hand so that your fingers are where the toes would be

Start A Patchwork Quilt

Patchwork is something which can be ongoing and, depending on the size of your chosen project, can be completed quite quickly or over a number of months or even years.

YOU WILL NEED
Scraps of fabric
Stiff card
Scissors
Pencil
Brown paper or thin card (old Christmas cards will suffice)
Pins
Needle
Thread
Material for backing completed patchwork

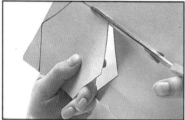

1 Cut out a hexagon from the stiff card. This is your template.

2 Place the hexagon onto the thin card or brown paper and draw round it several times.

3 Cut out the hexagons.

4 Pin the paper hexagons onto the scraps of material and cut around them, leaving a 2cm (¾in) margin of material all round.

5 Fold over the overlapping material and tack it onto the paper hexagon. Remove the pins (*see above right*).

6 Sew the patches together using fine overstitch.

7 Remove the tacking and paper.

8 Once you have completed the patchwork, sew it onto the backing material.

Disguises

There are many very simply ways in which you can disguise yourself. For example, practise moving in a different manner or walking in a different way. Try to disguise your voice by speaking in a different accent depending on who or what you would like to be. Change your shape by wearing clothes that

are too big for you or wearing lots of them to pad yourself out. Strap a small cushion to your middle and cover it with a tight T-shirt to give yourself an instant beer belly.

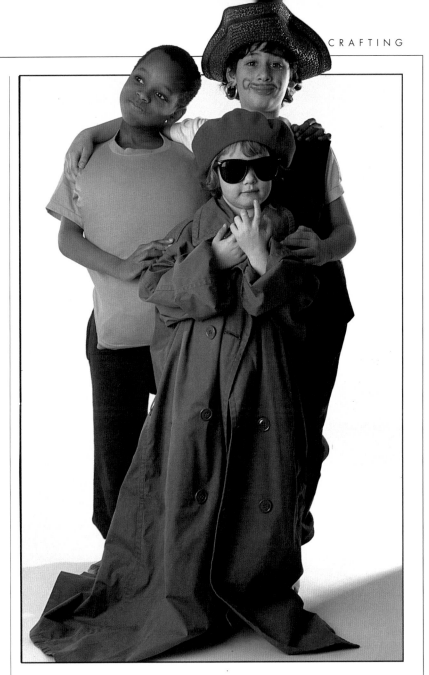

Disguising Your Face

Try making yourself a beard and a moustache from wadding. Experiment with face paints to see how you can change your appearance. Use different shades of foundation to change the hue of your skin and try to change the natural expression of your mouth.

CHAPTER FOUR

FUN WITH FOOD

We all like food and I have included some very easy items in this section of the book. The youngest children can have a go at decorating biscuits with icing and sweets to make biscuit faces. The longest sandwich in the world is a popular item and simple to make. There are healthy foods to make such as fresh fruit salad as well as less healthy, but always enjoyable, toffee apples and sweets. Some of the recipes don't require cooking, but those which do need adult supervision to make sure things don't go wrong. An adult should also supervise when knives are being used. Always make sure you have the ingredients before starting a recipe.

Pizza Faces

Surprise your family by offering to prepare lunch or supper. Pizzas are quick and easy to make if you use a scone mix for the base instead of dough.

YOU WILL NEED
225g (8oz) self-raising flour
Pinch of salt
50g (2oz) margarine
150ml (¼ pint) milk

For the topping
Tomato purée
Onions
Peppers
Tomatoes
Sweetcorn
Salami
Anchovies
Olives
Grated cheese

Equipment
Mixing bowl
Metal spoon
Rolling pin
Baking tray

1 Turn on the oven and preheat to 200°C (400°F) or Gas mark 6.

2 Sift the flour and salt into a mixing bowl.

3 Chop the margarine into pieces and rub into the flour until the mixture resembles fine bread-crumbs.

4 Stir in the milk until you have a soft but not sticky dough.

5 Roll out the dough to a thickness of 1cm (½ in) and form into a round shape approximately 30cm (12in) in diameter.

6 Spread the base with tomato purée and add the topping of your choice. Sprinkle with grated cheese.

7 Make a pizza face by using sliced pepper for the eyes, a mushroom for the nose and a piece of salami for the mouth.

8 Place pizza on a baking tray and bake for approximately 25 minutes.

Boiled Egg Mice

Turn some hard-boiled eggs into mice!

YOU WILL NEED
6 eggs
Lettuce
12 raisins
Brown sauce
Chopping board
Round-ended knife

1 Hard boil the eggs.

2 Allow the eggs to cool and peel off the shells.

3 Cut a small sliver off the side of each egg so that it will sit on a plate without rolling over.

4 Cut long tails and little triangular ears from the lettuce.

5 Cut slits in the sides of the eggs and insert the lettuce ears.

6 Make similar slits for the tails.

7 Dip the end of the eggs in some sauce for the noses and use raisins for the eyes.

8 Serve on a bed of grated cheese.

Popcorn

Popcorn is cheap and fun to make – it is also delicious eaten warm.

YOU WILL NEED
Popping corn
Cooking oil
Deep saucepan with a lid
Salt or Sugar

1 Pour a little oil into the saucepan, just enough to cover the base.

2 Place the saucepan on the hob and heat up the oil.

3 Place a couple of hand-fuls of corn in the saucepan and put the lid on.

4 Shake the pan to ensure the corn is covered in oil and is not sticking to the saucepan.

5 When you hear the corn starting to pop, shake the pan a little. Keep shaking the pan at intervals, while the popping continues.

6 The corn is cooked when the popping stops. Shake salt onto the corn for a savoury taste and sugar if a sweet taste is preferred.

Lemonade

This is how to make real lemonade which is very refreshing on a hot summer's day.

YOU WILL NEED
4 lemons
4 tbsp castor sugar
Water

Equipment
A pint jug
Lemon squeezer
Sharp knife

1 Cut the lemons in half with a sharp knife.

2 Squeeze the juice from the lemons using a lemon squeezer.

3 Pour the juice into the pint jug.

4 Add the sugar and enough boiling water to dissolve it and stir well.

5 Fill the jug with cold water and put the lemonade in the fridge until chilled. Serve with ice.

The Longest Sandwich In The World

This makes a good substantial lunch very quickly, using any available filling in the fridge.

YOU WILL NEED
French loaf
Butter or margarine
Fillings (cheese, ham, salami, egg, lettuce, cucumber, etc., for a savoury sandwich; or fruits, jam, etc. for a sweet sandwich)

1 Cut the french stick lengthways and butter it.

2 Add the sweet or savoury fillings you have selected.

Alternatives
● Start with a savoury filling at one end and finish with a sweet filling at the other to make a two-course meal in one sandwich!
● Fill with grated cheese, tomatoes and onion and bake in a preheated oven 180°C (350°F) or Gas mark 4) for about 15 minutes. Serve hot.

Burfi

Burfi is a very sweet Indian dessert which tastes great after a curry which it complements wonderfully.

YOU WILL NEED
3 tbsp chopped almonds
2 cups dessicated coconut
4 tbsp sugar

Equipment
Baking tray
Saucepan
Wooden spoon

1 Grease the baking tray.

2 Brown the almonds under a hot grill. Stir occasionally making sure that they do not burn.

3 Put the coconut and sugar in a thick bottomed pan and place it over a gentle heat. Stir it all the time to prevent it sticking, burning or browning.

4 Add the browned almonds.

5 Pour the mixture into the greased baking tray and leave to cool.

Fruit Salad

The best time to make this is in the summer when there is a plentiful selection of cheap fruits available.

YOU WILL NEED
A mixture of fruits that are in season
Lemon
Fruit juice (preferably apple)

Equipment
Bowl
Sharp knife

1 Peel and chop up the fruit, removing any pith and pips. If you do this over a plate you will not lose any of the juice.

2 Put all fruit into a bowl.

3 Squeeze the juice of the lemon over the fruit.

4 Add just enough apple juice to cover the fruit.

5 Serve by itself or with some cream.

Biscuit Faces

You can turn almost any kind of food, sweet or savoury, into a face. Biscuits are particularly good to use as they are usually round like a face, although you can use baked potatoes, pizzas, rolls, cakes and fruit.

YOU WILL NEED
Water biscuits, cream crackers or Ritz biscuits for savoury snacks
Rich tea or digestives for sweet snacks

Sweet face decorations
Tubes of readymade icing
Glacé cherries
Jellied fruit
A selection of sweets such as dolly mixtures, liquorice allsorts or smarties
Hundreds and thousands

Savoury face decorations
Butter or margarine
Marmite
Cream cheese
A selection of toppings such as salami, carrots, red or green peppers, cucumber, cheese, cottage cheese, miniature gherkins, raisins, tomatoes, olives, sweetcorn or anchovies

Sweet Biscuit Faces

Decorate the biscuits with tubes of readymade icing and sweets (*see right*).

Savoury Biscuit Faces

1 Spread some of the biscuits with cream cheese, butter or margarine. If you want to make dark faces, mix the spread with marmite. Leave other biscuits

plain and use the spread to stick the features onto the biscuits.

2 Use slices of olives, carrots, gherkins, or cocktail onions for the eyes.

3 Use grated carrot or cheese, or cut some salami into strips, for the hair. Cucumber, tomatoes, sweetcorn, green or red peppers could also be used effectively.

4 Use similar strips of a different ingredient to make the nose, mouth and eyebrows.

5 Make some faces sad, others happy and give them all different characteristics – add beards made from cottage cheese, for example, or an anchovy moustache, or cucumber ears.

Gingerbread Biscuits

This is a traditional recipe and shows how to make gingerbread men and women – something everyone should have a go at at some stage in their lives.

YOU WILL NEED
250g (10oz) self-raising flour
1 tbsp ground ginger
75g (3oz) margarine or butter
125g (5oz) golden syrup
125g (5oz) brown sugar
2 tbsp milk
Plain flour (for flouring the work surface)
A little margarine
Tube of ready-made icing
Sweets

Equipment
Sieve
Large bowl
Wooden spoon
Rolling pin
Baking tray
Gingerbread men cutters (optional)

1 Turn on the oven and preheat to 180°C (350°F) or Gas mark 4.

2 Sift the flour and ground ginger into the bowl. Rub the margarine into the flour using only your fingertips.

3 Mix the syrup, sugar and milk together in a bowl and add to the dry ingredients. Mix with a wooden spoon to form a dough.

4 Lightly flour your work surface and roll out the dough so that it is about 5cm (2in) thick all over.

5 Put the dough in the fridge for half an hour to harden.

6 Grease the baking tray.

7 Take the dough out of the fridge and cut out the biscuit shapes or gingerbread people. Place these on the baking tray leaving gaps between them so that the dough can spread.

8 Bake in the oven for about 15 minutes or until the gingerbread is a golden brown colour.

9 Place on a wire tray and leave to cool.

10 When cool decorate with the tube of icing and sweets.

Peppermint Creams

Peppermint creams are always popular with children and grown-ups. They can be made into mice or frogs for children and plain circles for adults, all of which make wonderful gifts.

YOU WILL NEED
2 egg whites
500g (1lb) icing sugar
Peppermint essence
Food colouring (pink or green is traditional)
Silver balls
Pink embroidery thread or string

Equipment
Mixing bowl
Metal spoon
Rolling pin

1 Separate the egg whites from the yolks. (Save the yolks for something else.)

2 Beat the whites until they are stiff and frothy.

3 Sieve the icing sugar into the egg whites and add the peppermint essence.

4 Beat the mixture until it reaches a stiff consistency.

5 If you wish to colour the mixture, add a few drops at this point and beat in well.

6 Roll out the mixture on a board covered with icing sugar and cut into rounds or mould into animal shapes.

7 Use the silver balls to make eyes for the animals and the thread or string for their tails.

Toffee Apples

Toffee apples are always a great treat and are good to eat while standing round bonfires especially on Guy Fawkes night.

YOU WILL NEED
8 apples
8 wooden skewers
150ml (¼ pint) water
350g (14oz) granulated sugar
175g (7oz) golden syrup
1 tsp vanilla essence
Saucepan

1 Wash and dry the apples.

2 Push a skewer in at the stalk end of each apple.

3 Put the water, syrup, sugar and vanilla essence into the saucepan and heat slowly until the sugar dissolves.

4 Bring to the boil and cover.

5 Cook for two minutes and uncover.

6 Boil for a further seven minutes without stirring. The toffee is ready when you can drop a teaspoonful of the mixture into cold water and it becomes brittle.

7 Swirl each apple in the toffee and leave to stand on a buttered dish.

Uncooked Chocolate Cake

Make this for tea today – it is scrumptious.

YOU WILL NEED
100g (4oz) butter
100g (4oz) dark chocolate
2 tbsp golden syrup
225g (8oz) digestive biscuits
Greased baking tin
Plastic bag
Rolling pin
Saucepan

1 Melt the butter, chocolate and syrup gently in the saucepan. Do not boil.

2 Put the biscuits into the plastic bag and crush them with the rolling pin.

3 Combine the biscuit crumbs with the other ingredients and press the mixture into the greased baking tray.

4 Leave it to set.

5 Cut into squares and eat.

69

Coffee and Butterscotch Fudge

Coffee and butterscotch fudge is easy to make and quite delicious.

YOU WILL NEED
100g (4oz) marshmallows
2 tbsp whipping cream
3 level tsp instant coffee powder
50g (2oz) soft light brown sugar
50g (2oz) butter
100g (4oz) icing sugar (sifted)

Equipment
Small tin or dish (about 15cm (6in) square)
Small saucepan

1 Grease the small tin or dish.

2 Put the marshmallows in a small saucepan with one tablespoon of the cream and the coffee powder and melt over a low heat.

3 Put the rest of the cream, brown sugar and butter into another saucepan and heat gently until the sugar dissolves.

4 Increase the heat and boil for five minutes.

5 Remove from the heat and add the melted marshmallow mixture and the sifted icing sugar.

6 Pour the mixture into the prepared tin and leave to set.

7 Cut the fudge into squares and store in an airtight tin or eat at once!

Shortbread

If you wish to make a gift of your shortbread then decide what shape it is going to be so that you can find a suitable box to decorate (*see page 49*).

YOU WILL NEED
100g (4oz) plain flour
50g (2oz) ground rice
50g (2oz) caster sugar
Pinch of salt
100g (4oz) butter

Equipment
Bowl
Sieve
Greaseproof paper
Rolling pin
Baking tray
Fork
Knife
Wire rack

1 Preheat the oven to 180°C (350°F) or Gas mark 4.

2 Sieve together the flour, ground rice, caster sugar and salt in a bowl.

3 Rub in the butter making sure you lift the mixture as you do so to ensure the mixture is light and airy. Keep rubbing the butter in until the mixture resembles fine breadcrumbs.

4 Then knead it together to form a ball. Place it on a piece of greaseproof paper and roll it into a 20cm (8in) round about 1cm (½in) thick.

5 Place it on the baking tray.

6 Pinch the edges, prick the middle all over with a fork and mark it into approximately eight sections with a knife.

7 Bake in the oven for about 45 minutes or until the shortbread is firm to touch and a light, golden brown.

8 Put it on a wire rack to cool. Cut the shortbread into the marked pieces before it completely cools.

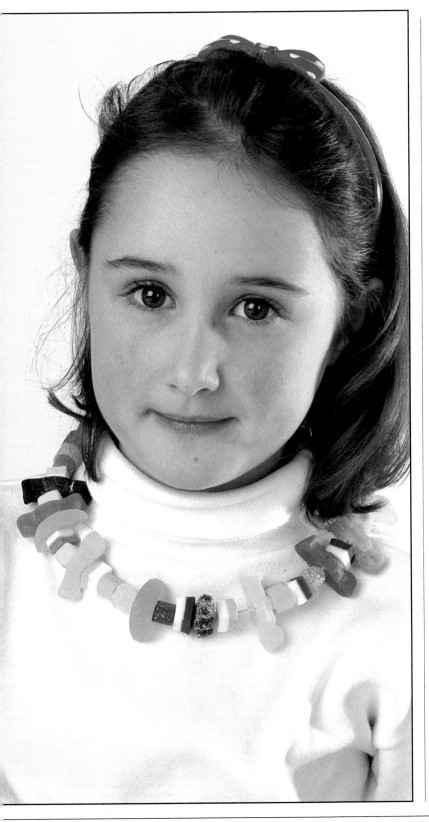

Jewellery From Sweets

Jewellery made from sweets can be very attractive and always sparks off amusing comments.

YOU WILL NEED
Miniature sweets (liquorice allsorts, dolly mixtures)
Needle
Thread
Embroidery thread

1 Buy a packet of miniature sweets and select which you are going to use to make a necklace or bracelet.

2 Pierce holes through each individual sweet with the needle.

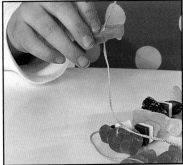

3 Thread them onto shirring elastic and tie loosely round your neck.

4 To preserve the necklace or bracelet, leave the sweets to dry out for about a week.

CHAPTER FIVE

GROWING THINGS

Apart from the wild-flower garden which could be a wild-flower window box or container, all the growing ideas are on a small scale. Some of them, such as mustard and cress, produce results very quickly, others take a little longer. It is fun to keep seeds and pips from fruits you have eaten and plant them to see which will grow first. If you want large quantities of mustard and cress, plant the seeds on a saucer. If you wish to grow some mustard and cress hair, plant the seeds in an old egg shell and decorate it with a face.

Mustard and Cress

Growing mustard and cress is very straightforward but will take one to two weeks before it is ready to eat.

YOU WILL NEED
Kitchen cloth, absorbent kitchen roll, or flannel
Saucer or small pie dish
Mustard and cress seeds

1 Put the kitchen cloth, absorbent kitchen roll or flannel in the sauce or dish.

2 Dampen the absorbent material.

3 Sprinkle the seeds onto the surface.

4 Keep the seeds in the dark until the shoots begin to grow then move them into the light remembering to keep it moist.

5 The mustard and cress will be ready to eat in about two weeks.

Eggheads

An alternative, fun idea, is to grow mustard and cress in an empty eggshell and decorate it with a face.

YOU WILL NEED
Hard-boiled eggs
Felt-tip pens
Mustard and cress seeds
Cotton wool

1 Remove egg from the shell and draw face on the empty shell.

2 Place a piece of moist cotton wool inside the egg.

3 Sprinkle on the seeds and wait for them to sprout a crop of mustard and cress hair. Remember to keep the cotton wool moist.

Bean Sprouts

It takes about a week for the bean sprouts to grow fully, so don't expect instant results.

YOU WILL NEED
2 tbsp mung or aduki beans
Large clean jam jar
Absorbent kitchen cloth or a piece of muslin
Elastic band
Warm water

1 Put 2 tbsp of the mung or aduki beans in the jar.

2 Cover the jar with the kitchen cloth or muslin and seal tightly with the elastic band.

3 Pour enough warm water through the cloth or muslin to cover the beans and leave them overnight to soak.

4 The next day empty the water from the jar, leaving the cloth in place.

5 Place the jar in a warm place such as an airing cupboard.

6 Pour warm water over the beans and drain it off morning and evening for the next few days. By the end of the week you have a jar full of crunchy beansprouts. They taste delicious in salads or sandwiches.

Grow A Tree In A Pot

Try and collect some seeds during the autumn months which you can then plant during the spring. Growing a tree in a pot is a good way to study a tree's growth and also means that if you don't have a garden you can still grow something. Some seeds, such as acorns and conkers, are large and contain a lot of stored food which provides the plant with nourishment when it begins to germinate. A tree in a pot will not grow as fast or as large as a tree in its natural habitat.

YOU WILL NEED
Pot for planting seeds (as large as possible)
Seeds
Compost or soil taken from the area in which you found the seeds
Label
Pencil
Notebook

1 Fill the plant pot about three-quarters full of the compost or soil. Place the seed on the surface and cover with a layer of soil.

2 Label each pot with the name of the seed and the date of planting.

3 Keep a notebook and chart the progress of the tree's growth.

4 Remember to water the tree and keep the soil moist.

Cat Grass

You can buy cat-grass seeds from pet shops as well as garden centres. Your cat will enjoy eating the results.

YOU WILL NEED
Cat grass seeds
Small flower pot
Saucer
Potting compost
Water

1 Fill the pot approximately three-quarters full of compost.

2 Sprinkle the seeds and cover with another layer of compost.

3 Stand the pot on the saucer and keep the compost moist.

Wild-Flower Garden

Growing wild flowers can produce a very attractive garden and may attract all sorts of wildlife to your garden, but it must be remembered that it is illegal to dig up or pick wild flowers growing in public places.

YOU WILL NEED
Packets of wild-flower seeds (or ask other gardeners to give you their unwanted plants – which they may consider to be weeds)
Area of garden designated for your use
Trowel

1 Clear your patch of unwanted materials such as weeds and large stones.

2 Decide where each seed or plant will go remembering to plant the taller specimens at the back, or in the middle if it is a round plot.

3 Plant the seeds according to the instructions on the packet.

4 Every week, check for weeds and remove them while watching the progress of your seeds.

5 When fully grown some of the flowers could be dried or pressed and used to make a flower arrangement.

Grow A Busy Lizzie

Busy Lizzies come in all sorts of colours. Their long, hanging, flowering stems make attractive indoor and outdoor plants.

YOU WILL NEED
Busy Lizzie seeds
Pot for inside or outside
Soil

1 Plant the seeds outside in a sunny position in the late spring. Cover the seeds with a thin layer of soil.

2 When the seedlings are 2–3cm (1in) high, transplant them into pots and either bring them inside or leave outside.

3 Remember, particularly if the plants are inside, they will need plenty of water.

4 Once established, Busy Lizzies grow anywhere so you may wish to take some cuttings. You could even try to sell them.

Grow A Cactus

Cacti are great to grow as they survive very well if you forget to water them!

YOU WILL NEED
Potting compost
Coarse sand
Seed tray
Cactus seeds
Sticky labels
Lolly sticks
Pencil

1 Spread a mixture of the potting compost and coarse sand in the seed tray.

2 Sprinkle the seeds in rows in the tray.

3 Write on the labels what sort of cactus it is and stick them to the lolly sticks.

4 Place the lolly sticks at the end of each row.

5 Water the seeds, cover and keep warm. They will need to be left for about a year to reach maturity but you will see some growth before that.

Grow A Herb Garden

You can make a herb garden even if you do not have a garden by simply planting a window box. Herbs make great gifts so if the garden is successful you can use the produce in your own cooking and to give away as presents. Start with the easiest herbs to grow which are: mint, thyme, marjoram and chives.

YOU WILL NEED
Mint, thyme, marjoram and chive seeds
Pots, window box or a plot of garden
Soil

1 Place the soil or compost into your chosen container.

2 Plant the seeds according to the instructions on the packet. (If planting mint it may be advisable to plant it in a contained space as it can very easily take over the whole garden).

3 Remember to water the seeds and to thin them out as they grow.

4 When fully grown, pick the herbs and dry them out.

Initialled Fruit

If you would like to see your initials growing, draw them on an apple, pear, marrow, pumpkin or other smooth-skinned fruit or vegetable while it is still growing. Very carefully cut out the letters, removing the skin. Do not cut too deeply. Leave the fruit or vegetable to grow and watch your initials as they grow – it is almost like watching a patterned balloon being inflated. Another way to grow your initials is to cut them out of masking tape and stick them to the fruit or vegetable. When it has ripened remove the tape to reveal your initials.

77

Bulbs for Christmas

Plants make good Christmas presents – you just have to remember to plant them in the autumn!

YOU WILL NEED
Hyacinth, daffodil or crocus bulbs (if planted in September or October they will flower for Christmas)
Container (lined basket, pot or hyacinth glass)
Bulb fibre

1 Wet some bulb fibre and squeeze it out.

2 Place this fibre in the container.

3 Arrange bulbs on the fibre and then add more fibre until just the tips of the bulbs are showing through.

4 Place the container in a dark place, keeping them moist.

5 When shoots appear, bring the pot into the light to continue growing. (If growing hyacinth bulbs in a hyacinth glass, add some charcoal to the bottom and fill the glass with water until it just touches the bulb. Then follow steps 4 and 5 above.)

Grow Your Own Crystals

Growing your own crystals is fun and the results can be very impressive. We chose to grow a copper sulphate crystal, but alum or salt crystals produce equally beautiful results.

YOU WILL NEED
Newspaper
Tablespoon
Clean glass jar
Alum, copper sulphate or salt crystals
Bowl of hot water
Long piece of thread or string
Paper clip
Piece of card

1 Put the spoon in the jar and fill it two thirds full of hot water. The metal spoon will absorb some of the heat from the water and stop the jar from cracking.

2 Remove the spoon.

3 Put two tablespoons of

alum, copper sulphate or salt crystals into the water and stir until it dissolves.

4 Stand the jar in a bowl of hot water (to keep the water in the jar hot). Add more crystals, stirring each spoonful until it dissolves (*see below*).

5 Keep adding more until it no longer dissolves. The solution is now saturated.

6 Tie one end of the thread to the paperclip and the other end through a slit in the card. Knot the thread so it does not slip through.

7 Drop the paperclip into the water solution in the jar and lie the card across the top. The paperclip should hang about half-way down the solution.

8 Leave the jar for a few days. As the water evaporates crystals form around the paper clip.

9 Remove the paper clip from the jar and select the biggest crystal.

10 Tie a piece of cotton around the crystal and thread the other end through the card.

11 Suspend the crystal in the solution as before.

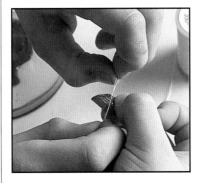

12 As the solution evaporates so the crystal will grow.

13 You may have to dissolve more crystals in the solution to keep it saturated, otherwise your crystal will begin to dissolve instead of grow.

Plant An Underwater Garden

Make an underwater garden in an old fishtank or goldfish bowl. Cover the bottom with a 2cm (¾in) layer of sand, then some compost and follow this with another 2cm (¾in) layer of sand. Fill the container with water and leave to settle. Buy some underwater plants from a local pet shop and collect some attractive pebbles and shells. When your plants are properly rooted, buy some water snails to keep the water clean.

CHAPTER SIX

OUTDOOR PURSUITS

There are activities for both summer and winter, for good and poor weather. You do not need a garden for the activities, any open space, such as a park or common, will do. Some of the activities can be solitary pursuits, for others you will need a group of friends. All are suitable for both country and city dwellers, in fact you may be surprised to find out just how much urban wildlife there is. So don't assume you need to live in the country to go tracking, to collect a spider's web or to foretell the weather.

Semaphore

Teach yourself semaphore and you will be able to communicate with a friend over a long distance.

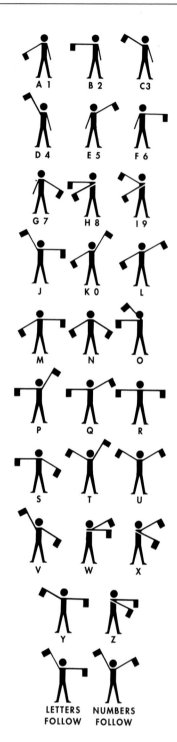

YOU WILL NEED
2 dusters, handkerchiefs or kitchen cloths
2 pieces of dowelling cane or rolled up newspaper
2 copies of the diagram on the right
Glue

1 Glue your chosen fabric to the pieces of dowelling, cane or rolled up newspaper.

2 Using semaphore code (*see right*) send messages to a friend who you can see but cannot hear.

Animal Tracks

You can look for animal tracks in the country or, if you live in a city, in parks. Below are some tracks made by different animals. You could keep a notebook and record which prints you find on what days and where. Dogs of various breeds will make different tracks and after a time you will be able to identify them.

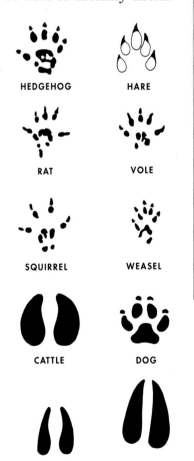

HEDGEHOG   HARE

RAT   VOLE

SQUIRREL   WEASEL

CATTLE   DOG

SHEEP   FALLOW DEER

Foretell The Weather

Amaze your friends by forecasting the weather!

The following indicate good weather:
- fir cones opening (they close when the weather is going to be bad),
- seed heads (such as dandelion clocks) opening,
- a heavy dew first thing in the morning.

The following indicate bad weather:
- fungus on tree trunks becoming moist and sticky,
- cattle and sheep standing at the sheltered end of their fields with their tails facing into the wind.
- your hair becoming curlier,
- the scent of flowers becoming stronger,
- the appearance of snail trails.

Collect A Spider's Web

A spider's web is a beautiful thing and must not be disturbed if it is still being used. It is possible, however, to mount and frame a web so that it can be kept. The best time to find a spider's web is in the early morning when they are often covered in dew.

YOU WILL NEED
Clear glue (wallpaper paste is quite good)
A sheet of black paper approximately 40cm (16in) square
Stiff card cut to the same size
A piece of glass cut to the same size
Picture frame clips

CAT   RABBIT

BADGER   FOX

1 Coat the black paper in clear glue.

2 Place the paper gently behind the web and it will stick to the glue.

3 Cut the edges of the web so that it fits the paper perfectly.

4 When the glue has dried lie the spider's web picture on the card and cover it carefully with the glass.

5 Fix together with the clips.

Throw the Wellie

This is a good outdoor game but needs quite a lot of space.

YOU WILL NEED
Old tyres or hoops
Wellington boots
Chalk

1 Chalk one of the following numbers on each side of the tyres or hoops: 10, 20, 50, 100 (if you want to score).

2 Scatter the tyres or hoops about the garden or open space.

3 Each person then takes a turn to try and throw their wellie into one of the tyres or hoops. Once you have succeeded you aim for another one and so on.

4 Add the scores up as you go along and the person with the highest score wins.

Two Ball Football

This is a silly game and great fun. The rules are the same as for ordinary football but you play with two balls. If both balls go through the goal posts at the same time they are both counted.

Clock Golf

Clock golf is a good game to play on the beach.

YOU WILL NEED
Sandy beach
Spade
Bats
Tennis balls

1 Dig a small hole in some damp sand using a spade.

2 Draw a circle around the hole with a radius of 4 metres (4 yards).

3 Mark numbers 1 to 12 around the outer edge of the circle as if it were a clock face.

4 The players start at number one and, using bats or sticks, try to hit a ball into the central hole with as few hits as possible.

5 Each player works his or her way round the clock hitting the ball into the hole from each number. The player who has made the least number of shots having worked their way round the clock is the winner.

Garden Hose Game

This is a good game to play on a hot day when there is nothing else to do. Collect some friends together and put on your swimsuits. You will have a lot of fun squirting water at each other. You will also keep cool and water the garden at the same time.

● Check there isn't a hosepipe ban operating in your area.

Make Your Own Assault Course

Find an open piece of ground and set up your own assault course. Try to make it as inventive and as demanding as you can depending on the ages of the children involved. Here are some suggestions for activities you might like to incorporate into your course.

- Climb through a hanging tyre
- Crawl through a standing tyre
- Throw balls into a bucket from a set distance.
- Run along a board (supported on a couple of bricks or telephone directories)
- Jump along in a sack
- Run with an egg and spoon
- Run on stilts
- Do a cartwheel and somersault to finish the course

Tracking

Play a tracking game with your friends. Split up into pairs or small groups and take turns to set off ten minutes or so before the other pair or group, leaving a trail for them to follow.

Below are some of the signs you might like to use but, before you start, make sure everyone knows what the different signs mean.

Remember to stick to safe areas and to keep the trails fairly short. Arrange to meet back at the base after a fixed amount of time (twenty minutes or so) has passed, even if you haven't completed the search.

GO THIS WAY

DO NOT GO THIS WAY

6 PACES IN THIS DIRECTION

GO ON TO CROSSROADS

WE HAVE SEPARATED

WE HAVE GONE HOME

CHAPTER SEVEN

EASTER AND CHRISTMAS IDEAS

Festive times provide a good excuse for making and doing a whole range of activities with all the family, however young or old. We give you lots of ideas for Easter and Christmas, including dressing up as a Christmas tree, making presents and making your own gift wrap. Any of the growing projects may also be given as Christmas presents. Convert the Easter egg hunt into a Christmas hunt by wrapping tiny presents and hiding those instead of the Easter eggs. This can be done inside or outside depending on the weather.

Decorated Easter Eggs

Decorating eggs for Easter is a very festive activity and one that all age groups will enjoy.

YOU WILL NEED
Eggs (one or two per child)
Onions cut into quarters
Red cabbage
Wool
Wax crayons or felt-tip pens
Glue
Saucepans
Water

1 Boil the eggs for five minutes or until they are hard. Alternatively, older children can 'blow' raw eggs by making a little hole at either end of the egg with a pin and blowing out the contents into a bowl.

2 Place the onion plus skin in a saucepan and cover with water. Bring to the boil and simmer for five minutes to extract the colour from the onion. This will create a yellow dye. To make a red dye boil some chopped red cabbage for five minutes. Allow both dyes to cool.

3 Use the wax crayons to make a pattern on the eggs and then immerse them in the dye of your choice.

4 Remove the eggs after an hour. All the areas except those covered by the wax will have been coloured by the dye.

Alternatives
● Cover the egg with glue and wind some wool around it to make a pattern. Immerse it in the dye for an hour. Remove the wool, when it is completely dry, and reveal the pattern.

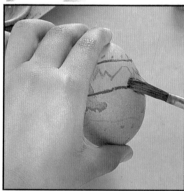

● Make faces or patterns by drawing directly onto the egg using felt-tip pens or paint. Glue on pieces of wool to make the hair or wind it round the egg to make a hat.

Easter Egg Hunt

This is a quick and fun game to play with the added bonus of a chocolate prize at the end!

YOU WILL NEED
Baskets (one per child)
Small chocolate eggs with different coloured foil wrappings

1 Hide a set number of eggs in the house or garden.

2 Each child is given a basket in which he or she will collect their eggs.

3 Tell each child which colour they are responsible for collecting and then send them off to look for the eggs. Alternatively, you could ask each child to collect one of each colour.

Marbled Eggs in an Egg-Noodle Basket

These eggs look very attractive especially when served sitting on a nest of egg noodles.

YOU WILL NEED
6 eggs
Blue or green food colouring
Ice cubes
250g (10oz) packet of medium egg noodles
Saucepan
Slotted spoon
Bowl
Colander

1 Place the eggs in a pan and cover with cold water.

2 Bring to the boil and simmer for three minutes.

3 Remove the eggs very carefully from the water using the slotted spoon.

4 Add two teaspoons of food colouring to the water so it becomes quite dark in colour.

5 Return the eggs to the water and cook for a further six minutes.

6 Place three or four ice cubes in a bowl of cold water and add one teaspoon of food colouring.

7 Plunge the eggs into the coloured iced water and leave for ten minutes. Meanwhile cook the egg noodles.

8 Bring a large saucepan of water to the boil and drop the noodles into this.

9 Remove from the heat but leave the noodles in the water for 6 minutes. Strain off the water using the colander.

10 Remove the eggs from the iced water and peel off the shells to reveal the wonderful marbled effect.

11 Arrange the noodles as a nest on a plate and place the eggs in the middle.

An Easter Chick

You can make many different animals once you know how to make pompoms. Here are some straightforward instructions on how to make an Easter chick.

YOU WILL NEED

2 pieces of card at least 30cm
(10in) square
2 pieces of card at least 20cm
(8in) square
Compass
Pencil
Scissors
Yellow wool
Scraps of yellow felt
Yellow pipe cleaners
Sequins
Fabric glue
Shirring elastic

1 Using a compass, draw a circle 30cm (10in) in diameter on both pieces of card.

2 Cut out both circles.

3 Cut out another circle from the centre of both pieces of card approximately 7.5cm (3in) in diameter.

4 Place the two pieces of card together and tie them together by winding the yellow wool round and round through the hole in the middle. Continue this until all the card has been covered with a thick layer of wool and the hole in the middle has been filled in.

5 Carefully cut through the wool on the outer edge of the circle. Keep one blade of the pair of scissors between the pieces of card.

6 Pull the pieces of card slightly apart and tie a piece of wool very tightly round the centre of the ball.

7 Completely remove the card and fluff out the wool to form a ball.

8 Make another pom-pom with a circle of card which has a diameter of 20cm (8in) by repeating steps 1–7.

9 Cut a diamond shape from the yellow felt and fold it in half. This is the chick's beak. Glue it in place on the smaller pom-pom.

10 Make two legs from the yellow pipe cleaners by twisting them round each other and through the centre of the larger pom-pom to hold them in place.

11 Glue two black sequins onto the head for eyes.

12 Fix the head to the body by tying together the threads round the middle of each pom-pom.

13 Suspend the chick from shirring elastic.

Alternatives

• Make an Easter bunny by following steps 1–7 but make three pom-poms, two using a brown or fawn-coloured wool and a much smaller one, using white wool, for the bunny's tail. Use white or brown pipe

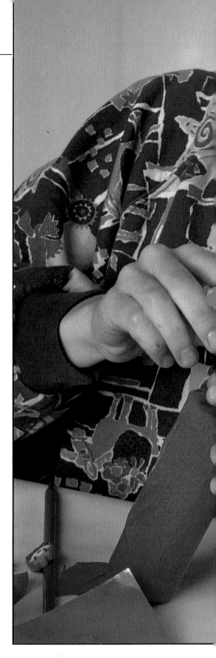

cleaners for the front legs and brown felt, cut into an oval with a point at one end, for the ears. Use sequins for the eyes and a patch of white felt, glued in place, for the nose. Make whiskers from short lengths of pipe cleaners glued into place.

Christmas Crackers

These paper crackers could be used for birthdays or Christmas. They also make good presents.

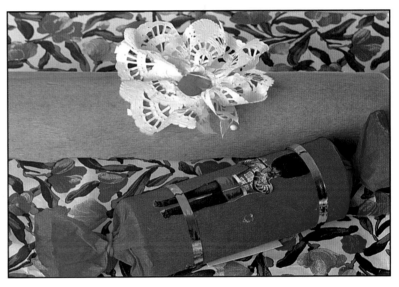

YOU WILL NEED
Crepe paper
Cardboard tube from a toilet roll
2 small rubber bands
A joke written on a small piece
of paper
Small sweets or gifts
Tissue paper hat
Doily
Old magazines
Scissors
Glue

1 Cut the crepe paper so that it is 10cm (4in) longer than the cardboard tube.

2 Put the tube in the middle of the crepe paper and glue it into place. Put the joke, sweets or gift and paper hat into the tube (*below left*).

3 Wrap the crepe paper around the tube until it completely covers the card.

4 Gather the crepe paper up at one end of the roll (*above left*) and secure it with an elastic band. Repeat at the other end.

5 Decorate the cracker with pieces of doily and paper cut from discarded magazines (*above*).

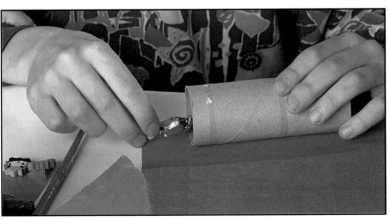

Christmas Tree Costume

YOU WILL NEED

Green fabric (it needs to measure the length of your body, i.e. from your neck to your ankles)
2 metres (2¼ yards) of green petticoat netting
Elastic
Christmas tree decorations
Thread
Needle
Pins
Tinsel

1 Turn over one edge of the green fabric (approximately 2cm (¾in) and sew with a running stitch. (This is to create a channel for the elastic to go through).

2 Cut the netting into lengthways strips approximately 10cm (5in) wide.

3 Gather the length of each piece of netting along one edge. Pin the netting onto the green fabric in rows. Sew with a running stitch and remove the pins.

4 Sew Christmas tree decorations onto the netting and fabric.

5 With right sides facing, sew down the side seam, leaving a gap at the top to insert the elastic.

6 Insert the elastic. Check that the costume fits and adjust the elastic accordingly before tying a knot.

7 Wear with a tinsel headband and stand in a pot covered with red crepe paper.

Paper Chains

Save some money by decorating the house with homemade decorations such as these attractive paper chains.

YOU WILL NEED

Coloured sugar paper or brightly coloured foil
Glue stick
Scissors

1 Cut the paper into strips (approximately 18×3cm (7×1in)).

2 Glue the ends of the first strip together.

3 Thread the next strip through the first and stick the ends of these together.

4 Repeat this process until you have a chain of the required length.

Salt Dough Christmas Tree Decorations

YOU WILL NEED

Salt Dough (*see recipe on page 32*)
Pastry cutters or make your own templates from card
Rolling pin
Skewer
Baking tray
Poster paint
Paintbrushes
Cotton

1 Preheat the oven to 180°C (350°F) or Gas mark 4.

2 Roll out the salt dough.

3 Cut out shapes using the pastry cutters or by cutting around your own cardboard templates.

4 Place the shapes onto the baking tray.

5 Make a hole with the skewer at the top of the shape so that you can thread some cotton through once the decoration is finished.

6 Add textures to the shape if you wish.

7 Place the dough shapes in the preheated oven. The length of time the dough will take to cook will depend on how large and how thick the shapes are. When the dough is hard remove from the oven.

8 Once it has cooled down, thread some cotton through the hole and decorate the shapes with paint and glitter.

Felt Christmas Tree Decoration

This is a quiet activity – much needed around this time of year!

YOU WILL NEED

Various pieces of different coloured felt
Wadding
Sequins, buttons, glitter and beads
Ribbon
Glue (Copydex is the best glue for sticking material)
Pins
Scissors
Needle
Thread
Tracing paper
Pencil
Pinking shears

1 Draw a Christmas tree shape onto the tracing paper.

2 Cut it out leaving a 1cm (½in) border all round.

3 Sandwich a piece of wadding between two pieces of green felt. Pin the tracing paper pattern to this.

4 Using running stitch, sew around the outline of the pattern making sure you go through the paper, felt and wadding.

5 Remove the pins and paper pattern.

6 Cut around the sewn shape using pinking shears. Do not cut too close to the stitching line – leave about 5mm (¼in) clear.

7 Decorate the tree with oddments of felt, buttons, bows, sequins and glitter.

going on the back of the tag once it has dried.

5 Punch a hole into the shape and thread some ribbon through the hole. If you want to make a kite gift tag then attach pasta bows to the ribbon to act as the tail.

Geometric Gift Tags

YOU WILL NEED
Cardboard in various colours
Pencil
Ruler
Scissors
Hole punch
Ribbon
Coloured sticky tape
Felt-tip pen

Gift Tags

Gift tags can be expensive to buy so here are a few ideas on how to make your own.

YOU WILL NEED
Thin card or paper
Narrow ribbon, embroidery silk or cotton thread
Felt-tip pens
Optional
Gingerbread man, teddy bear or other pastry cutters
Pasta bows
Poster paints
Hole punch

1 Draw an interesting shape onto the card or draw round a pastry cutter.

2 Decorate the shape with glue or glitter.

3 Cut out the shape.

4 Write the name of the person to whom the gift is

1 Draw a geometric shape, for example, a square, oblong or diamond, onto the card using a ruler.

2 Cut out the shape.

3 Use the felt-tip pens to decorate it with geometric designs or stick strips of coloured tape across the tag to make an interesting design.

4 Punch a hole in the top of the card and thread the ribbon through the hole. Attach it to the gift.

Gift Wrap

Here are some ideas for making your own Christmas gift wrap which can often be more attractive than shop-bought paper.

YOU WILL NEED
Newspaper
Oil-based paints (artists' oil paints work well)
Turpentine substitute
One saucer for each colour of paint
Large bowl of water (it needs to be large enough to take the size of paper you are working with)
Brush
Rubber gloves
Plain white paper

1 Cover the surface on which you are working with a lot of newspaper.

2 Squeeze a little colour onto a saucer and mix with a little turpentine.

3 Drop the colour onto the surface of the water and you will see that it floats.

4 Mix a second colour and add it to the water. Stir.

5 Put the rubber gloves on to protect your hands.

6 Hold the corners of your paper and place it on the surface of the water. The paint will adhere to the paper.

7 Lift the paper off quickly so that the colour does not run.

8 Leave it to dry.

9 Add more colours to the water and repeat steps 4–8.

10 Clean all the brushes and utensils with the turpentine.

Alternatives
● Wrap your presents in brown paper and tie with hairy, coloured string, wool or gold braid. If none of these are available, use bias binding and decorate it with small flowers or hearts.
● Cover brown paper with brightly coloured potato prints (*see page 18*) or use any of the ideas for creating textures (*on page 11*) to decorate the paper.
● Use simple stencils or draw round pastry cutters to make brightly coloured paper.

Index